IRON WILL

Inside the Invincible Mind
Of the
Navy SEAL

Navy SEAL Lessons for Becoming Unstoppable!

Table of Contents

Introduction

There exist, in our midst, men and women who achieve great physical feats, attain impossible goals, and perform to unimaginable levels. Often we may think that reaching the same sort of success is out of our reach. The truth is a bit more complex. I have written this book in an attempt to introduce you to the unique qualities that are at the core of a special breed of warriors known as the Navy SEALs. Many people are intrigued by the SEALs and what they do; dangerous, secretive missions in remote regions of the world. While there are many aspects of the Navy SEALs that are interesting and perhaps helpful for others to know about, the focus of this book is on the *mindset, attitude, traits and habits* that enable SEALs to consistently achieve success under the most daunting and dangerous circumstances imaginable.

Unlike what is often found in many other books, I do not wish to portray SEALs as demigods or otherwise perfect men. In my opinion, that portrayal is not only misleading, it perpetuates the misconception about the impossibility for regular people, or 'mere mortals,' to even attempt to emulate these exceptional warriors. The truth is that anyone, regardless of their age or physical capabilities, can develop the same levels of mental toughness, will power and resilience possessed by Navy SEALs, and the purpose of this book is to help you do just that!

A battle-hardened SEAL once told me, "There's a lot of hype and mystique associated with the SEAL community; the good news is that some of it is actually true!" What he meant was that although SEALs are not perfect men, they do strive for perfection in all that they do. They are not born with super-human talent and abilities; rather, they are transformed into supremely capable warriors through time-tested, continuous and highly-focused training and operational experiences. Most important of all – they become winners in the truest sense of the word. SEALs succeed, more often than not, largely because they have developed an invincible mindset and iron will that demands success in any situation and in any environment, no matter how challenging it may be. Not surprisingly, these are the same traits required of anyone aspiring to become a high-achiever in any walk of life.

This book will not provide you with great detail about combat operations or the training that transforms civilians into SEAL operators. It does, however, contain anecdotes and examples of SEAL operations, which have been carefully selected for their effectiveness in illustrating certain aspects of the mindset, mental approach and attitudes shared by members of the SEAL community. It also contains anecdotes about several SEALs that will help illustrate the invincible mindset common to members of this very special breed of warriors. My hope is that this book will cause you to assess your life and where you stand relative to the hopes, dreams and personal or professional goals you have or once had.

Although young men desiring to become SEALs or members of other special operations units will benefit greatly from reading this book, it is my belief that the vast majority of those who read it will never serve in the armed forces. This book was written for men and women of all ages and from all walks of life who are seeking to improve some aspect of their personal and professional lives, and who are wise enough to know that it is impossible to effect significant change in one's life without first changing one's current way of thinking.

America's Warrior Class

In many nations and societies, due to the constant conflict occurring during the Middle Ages and throughout history, a "warrior class" needed to exist. The warrior class – a group of men recognized for their skill in combat or waging war - was often the dominant factor in determining whether a nation, society or tribe survived or was eliminated from the face of the earth. As such, the warrior class was afforded great respect by royalty and the common citizenry, and the individual warrior was celebrated as being the ideal example of what all young males should aspire to become.

By the end of the 19th century, the concept of a warrior class or "military caste" had largely become an anachronism in most modern nations. Though the term "warrior" was still sometimes used, it was typically in reference to members of large, organized professional armies and naval forces comprised of civilians who were either conscripts or volunteers. These men left civilian life, served in the military forces for a period of time and then returned to civilian life to become members of society at large. In the ancient context, being a member of a warrior class meant that one was literally born into a class or caste of people whose sole purpose in life was to become a "man of arms" and serve the nation as a soldier – for life.

When America was established long ago, the Founding Fathers envisioned a nation protected by an army of private citizens led by military officers who followed the orders of elected or appointed civilian officials. These men were students of history and they felt that a true warrior class had often led to militaristic nations that seemed to engage in war and conquest as their primary reason for being.

America's Warrior Class

Over the years, America's armed forces have evolved from militias and small, relatively untrained organizations, to very large, highly trained and capable instruments of war that have no equal in today's world. But, despite the best intentions of the Founding Fathers and subsequent civilian and military leaders to prevent the existence of a warrior class in America – it does exist, and members of the Navy SEALs believe they are not only a part of it, but that they are truly the elite of the elite! Although it is rarely, if ever, discussed, every single SEAL feels that today's SEAL teams are the modern day Spartan warriors.

Any book written by or about SEALs (this one included!), will invariably contain references to "rites of passage" used by ancient warrior classes to ensure prospective warriors had the mental toughness and basic fighting skills required for the brutal combat of those eras. You'll note the prolific use of quotes attributed to notable warriors, leaders and philosophers of ancient Sparta, Athens, the Roman Empire and other significant "warrior nations." SEALs have the utmost respect for these ancient warriors, knowing that they were the very best fighters in the world at various points in history. Their training and selection methods, like those of the SEAL community, were quite rigorous and the standards were far higher than those of regular, conventional military forces.

The Rite of Passage

In the opinion of many, the entry-level training and selection course for today's SEAL team, the Basic Underwater Demolitions/SEAL (BUD/S) course is the most difficult selection course in the world – and is unequaled as a "rite of passage" to membership in a special operations unit. The Spartans had the Agoge – the crucible into which all young males were thrust and, if survived, were transformed into warriors worthy of representing Sparta. The Agoge was designed to make Spartan boys grow into fierce warriors and to instill in them patriotism, loyalty, obedience and comradeship. The SEALs have BUD/S, which is the only entry point into the SEAL community, with no exceptions. BUD/S is the Navy SEAL version of the Spartan Agoge and every man wearing the famous Trident insignia on his chest has survived this intense and often brutal selection process.

To fully understand the mentality of those who become Navy SEALs, you must reflect on what you've just read. Many thousands of honorable young Americans join the various branches of the U.S. military because they want to serve their country and hopefully, obtain skills and capabilities that can become valuable assets in the civilian world. The young men that join the U.S. Navy so they can get a shot at BUD/S do so with one purpose in mind: to become members of an elite warrior society – the SEAL Teams.

"There is nothing outside of yourself that can ever enable you to get better, stronger, richer, quicker, or smarter. Everything is within. Everything exists. Seek nothing outside of yourself."

~ Miyamoto Musashi. The Book of Five Rings

SEAL Ethos

As stated previously, the main objective of this book is to enable readers to learn about the mindset of SEALs, how they think and what their collective mental approach is when faced with challenges and obstacles. One cannot completely understand the SEAL mindset without first understanding the ethos of the SEAL community, the core values and beliefs that serve as the foundation for this special breed of warrior.

Let's begin by having a common understanding of the word *ethos*. As defined by the Merriam-Webster dictionary:

Ethos: *The distinguishing character, sentiment, moral nature, or guiding beliefs of a person, group, or institution.*

Several years ago, current and former members of the SEAL community collaborated on an effort to capture in writing the essence of America's frogmen. The results of their work can be seen below, in what is now referred to as the "Navy SEAL Ethos."

Navy SEAL Ethos

"In times of war or uncertainty there is a special breed of warrior ready to answer our Nation's call. A common man with an uncommon desire to succeed. Forged by adversity, he stands alongside America's finest special operations forces to serve his country, the American people, and protect their way of life. I am that man.

My Trident is a symbol of honor and heritage. Bestowed upon me by the heroes that have gone before, it embodies the trust of those I have sworn to protect. By wearing the Trident I accept the responsibility of my chosen profession and way of life. It is a privilege that I must earn every day. My loyalty to Country and Team is beyond reproach. I humbly serve as a guardian to my fellow Americans always ready to defend those who are unable to defend themselves. I do not advertise the nature of my work, nor seek recognition for my actions. I voluntarily accept the inherent hazards of my profession, placing the welfare and security of others before my own. I serve with honor on and off the battlefield. The ability to control my emotions and my actions, regardless of circumstance, sets me apart from other men. Uncompromising integrity is my standard. My character and honor are steadfast. My word is my bond.

We expect to lead and be led. In the absence of orders I will take charge, lead my teammates and accomplish the mission. I lead by example in all situations. I will never quit. I persevere and thrive on adversity. My Nation expects me to be physically harder and mentally stronger than my enemies. If knocked down, I will get back up, every time. I will draw on every remaining ounce of strength to protect my teammates and to accomplish our mission. I am never out of the fight.

We demand discipline. We expect innovation. The lives of my teammates and the success of our mission depend on me - my technical skill, tactical proficiency, and attention to detail. My training is never complete. We train for war and fight to win. I stand ready to bring the full spectrum of combat power to bear in order to achieve my mission and the goals established by my country. The execution of my duties will be swift and violent when required yet guided by the very principles that I serve to defend. Brave men have fought and died building the proud tradition and feared reputation that I am bound to uphold. In the worst of conditions, the legacy of my teammates steadies my resolve and silently guides my every deed. I will not fail."

Powerful words!

And, for the men who wear the Trident - they are truly words to live by!

"Such as are your habitual thoughts, such also will be the character of your mind; for the soul is dyed by the thoughts."

~ Marcus Aurelius

Introduction to SEAL Training

It would be difficult to truly grant SEALs their due admiration and awe without some knowledge of the rigorous training that they subject themselves to in order to join the ranks of the warriors who have come before them. However, as important as it is to know about their training, it is more important, for the purposes of this book, that you understand the mindset and the will power that is imperatively necessary in order to survive the rigors and demands of this intense training.

In this book we will cover only a basic introduction to the BUD/S training course and the selection process that takes place for all SEALs. If you are interested in learning about basic and advanced SEAL training in more detail, I encourage you to seek out one of the many SEAL-authored books that are available out in the market.

Naval Special Warfare Prep School

This eight-week course is located in Great Lakes, Illinois. It is the starting point for the vast majority of prospective SEALs. It begins right after the students graduate from the Navy recruit training and is supervised by active duty SEALs and other specialists associated with the SEAL community. The main emphasis of this course is physical fitness and preparing the students for the physical demands of BUD/S. Students that cannot meet certain standards of fitness are either retained for remedial instruction and development or dropped from the program.

BUD/S Orientation Course

Lasting approximately three weeks, this course is designed to orient students to the Naval Special Warfare Training Center at Coronado. They are exposed to the daily routine they will experience during Phase I of BUD/S, and they are issued some of the clothing and equipment they will use throughout the course. Physical training remains a major priority and the degree of difficulty of the daily workouts increases significantly.

BUD/S First Phase – Basic Conditioning

Simply put, the main goal of the seven week long phase is to weed out students who do not possess the commitment required to complete BUD/S. While all of the students have already met certain physical requirements and are capable of completing BUD/S in that aspect, history shows that about 75% of them do not possess the mental toughness and resolve necessary to graduate from the course and eventually serve as SEALs.

The weeding out process is achieved primarily through rigorous physical training and other evolutions designed to inflict fatigue, discomfort and high levels of mental stress upon the students. Most of the training evolutions are graded and the pass/fail standards are increased with the passing of each week. Phase I is the "meat grinder" of BUD/S and is responsible for the vast majority of the attrition experienced by each BUD/S class.

The big event in Phase I is the infamous "Hell Week" evolution, which consists of 5 ½ days of continuous physical training and other evolutions designed to exhaust the students and push them to the limits of physical and mental endurance. During a typical Hell Week, several dozen students will decide that they no longer desire to become SEALs and they will quit BUD/S.

BUD/S Second Phase – Combat Diving

This seven week phase is focused on teaching the students how to become basic combat swimmers. In order to accomplish this, a great amount of time is spent in the BUD/S training tank executing various techniques and tasks, predominantly underwater. Throughout this phase, the student will be subjected to many graded evolutions that get more difficult and stressful as each day passes. As one would expect, any student that has a fear of being underwater will be quickly identified by the instructors. Many SEALs describe this phase as being the most difficult part of BUD/S.

This phase is deemed quite challenging academically due to the great deal of classroom instruction associated with learning open and closed-circuit diving techniques. In addition to extensive work in the training tank, the students are continually graded on demanding physical training evolutions such as timed distance runs, timed runs of the obstacle course and open ocean swims.

BUD/S Third Phase – Land Warfare Training

This seven week long phase is where the students undergo detailed instruction on the firearms and explosives they will need to master as part of their SEAL training. Also, in addition to becoming proficient in the use of both, they will receive instruction and be evaluated in skills such as land navigation and small-unit tactics.

Most of the classroom instruction associated with this phase takes place at the BUD/S training compound. The final weeks of the phase are spent on San Clemente Island (also referred to as "The Rock"), which is located off the coast of southern California and where the SEALs maintain live fire and demolition ranges. Students run through a series of graded evolutions and practical application exercises during their time on the island.

Throughout this phase, the emphasis on physical training remains high; and standards and passing scores for timed runs, swims and the obstacle course are progressively elevated to ensure that the students find each subsequent week more demanding than the past one. Upon successful completion of this phase, the students will have achieved their immediate goal of graduating BUD/S. Even though at that point they are not yet officially considered SEALs, they can relax just a bit, knowing that the major barrier to earning their Trident insignia has been cleared.

SEAL Qualification Training

SEAL Qualification Training (SQT) is the twenty-six week "finishing school" for BUD/S graduates. It is designed to transform these basically-trained combat swimmers into fully qualified SEALs ready to join an operational unit. Students undergo advanced weapons training and extensive instruction in small unit tactics. They are exposed to advanced demolitions techniques and become more proficient at land navigation during both day and night operations.

During SQT the students become qualified in parachute operations; and they make both static line and free-fall jumps during this part of the curriculum. Also covered are the various types of communications equipment, along with the extensive medical skills and life-saving techniques that have proven essential during combat operations. This phase includes cold weather training in Alaska, as well as more extensive training in waterborne operations.

Upon the successful completion of SQT, students finally earn the right to wear the coveted Trident insignia. They are now fully-qualified Navy SEALs and will be assigned to an operational unit.

"It takes a little courage, and a little self-control. And some grim determination, if you want to reach the goal. It takes a great deal of striving, and a firm and stern-set chin. No matter what the battle, if you really want to win, there's no easy path to glory. There is no road to fame. Life, however we may view it, is no simple parlor game; but its prizes call for fighting, for endurance and for grit; for a rugged disposition that will not quit."

~ Navy SEAL Master Chief

The Purpose of BUD/S

Now that you have a basic understanding of the training pipeline all SEALs have to go through in order to become a fully qualified frogman, I want to add a bit more detail about BUD/S. If you can gain a deeper appreciation of BUD/S and what occurs there, you'll stand a better chance at understanding Navy SEALs. More importantly, you will gain a better understanding of the mindset and mental approach that encompasses the iron will that enables SEALs to do what they do best – produce exceptional results in exceptionally challenging environments and situations.

First, let's go over a couple of terms and definitions that will be useful to know as you continue reading. Within special operations units in the U.S. and around the world, the terms *training* and *selection* have two very distinct and different meanings.

A *training course* is one in which students are educated and trained in specific concepts, skills and techniques. For example, a SEAL attending the sniper course will learn the tactics and techniques associated with serving as a sniper.

A *selection course* is one that is designed to screen, test and evaluate students for certain physical and mental attributes. In most special operations units, candidates must first pass selection before they are allowed to receive any measurable amount of training.

BUD/S is a hybrid of these concepts. It is a training course, which means the students are actually learning some of the skills and techniques associated with serving as a SEAL. It is also a selection course, which means that there's much more involved in becoming a SEAL than learning and performing the skills and techniques previously mentioned – it is about meeting standards, written and unwritten, that are the hurdles one must clear in order to wear the Trident. I think it is obvious that the BUD/S evolution known as Hell Week is more geared toward selection versus training!

BUD/S will quickly weed out those who lack both the physical capability and the level of commitment needed to succeed as a SEAL. It usually takes longer, however, to identify and eliminate those who are physically capable of serving as SEALs and who truly want to do so, but are lacking the strength of will and mental toughness to serve as SEAL Team guys. Historically, those making it through Hell Week have a very high probability of making it through the entire pipeline and becoming SEALs, but it is a fact that some men who survive Hell Week ultimately fail to complete BUD/S. I once heard a BUD/S instructor say, "The millstone of BUD/S grinds slowly, but it grinds finely." I thought this to be a profound statement then, and still do today.

Men are very rarely dismissed from a BUD/S class; instead, they are continuously pushed to their mental and physical limits until some of them choose to quit the course. BUD/S is a course full of traditions, customs and rituals and even the act of quitting has evolved into a standardized routine. Quitting, or *dropping on request* is done through a public event called "Ringing Out," in which a man who has decided to quit rings a large brass bell three times and places his helmet on the deck alongside those of former classmates who have already exited the course. Men who ring out of BUD/S are not harassed or demeaned by the instructor staff. They are quickly removed from the training area and processed for orders to another duty station where they will complete their time in the Navy.

In the final analysis, BUD/S takes men possessing the raw aptitude and traits to serve as a frogman, and over time, develops them into men with a very powerful state of mind – an invincible mentality that is always focused on finding a way to succeed. BUD/S is all about instilling some of the fundamental core values of the SEAL community into the students. These core values include:

- Accomplishing the mission is all that matters.

- They don't hand out 2nd Place trophies in war.

- Whatever needs to happen, must be *made* to happen.

- Luck is good, but preparation is better.

- Never make excuses.

- One must never bring shame to the SEAL brotherhood.

In order to fulfill these values and deliver upon their promise, SEALs are put through an incredibly difficult trial that calls for an extraordinary amount of mental toughness. Although most SEALs possess mental toughness as they initiate this training, it is through strife, pain and perseverance that this mental fortitude is brought to the level needed for these men to successfully and effectively function in the scenarios that SEALs are invariably placed under.

If we take some of the same methods used by SEALs and apply them in our own quest for optimal performance in our lives, this mental toughness is a malleable clay that any one of us can mold into the masterpiece that will give us the needed edge in order to accomplish any goal.

"We must remember that one man is much the same as another, and that he is best who is trained in the severest school."

~Thucydides, 431–404 B.C.

Mental Toughness

It is a common misconception to think that mental toughness is an innate quality that some people are simply born with and others are not. I don't ascribe to this theory. Mental toughness can be learned and developed by anyone with the desire to do so.

Typically, mental toughness is developed in SEALs and other special operations personnel by means of prolonged periods of exceptionally demanding physical training and endurance-type events. These evolutions are designed to bring men to the limits of their physical capabilities (or what they believe them to be) in order to determine if they have the mental fortitude to push past the pain and emotional stress they are experiencing. Much of this is intended to replicate conditions and stress levels associated with combat operations.

Obviously, SEALs are required to possess exceptional physical strength and stamina in order to operate successfully. Few other occupations require the same level of physical fitness or prowess. Though, it is a fact that one has to possess a certain level of mental toughness in order to be considered exceptional or high-achieving in almost any field or occupation.

Airline pilots, entrepreneurs, emergency medical technicians, trial attorneys and stock traders are some examples of professions which require minimal physical strength or endurance, yet require high levels of mental toughness if one is to be successful. On a more personal level, people who are dealing with issues such as disease and poor health, obesity, substance abuse and addiction or challenging personal relationships also need to possess varying degrees of this quality if they are to overcome these problems and live a happy and successful life.

I think that if you ask any number of people for their definition of mental toughness, you'd get many different answers. This is exactly what happens even among SEALs and other special operators; they all know what it is they are describing, yet there is no common definition for it, at least, none that I am aware of.

Several years ago, a friend was pursuing a graduate degree at the Naval Postgraduate School in Monterey, California. The topic for his graduate thesis was mental toughness and its impact on special operators. He surveyed several dozen SEALs and similar numbers of members of Army Special Forces, Marine Corps Reconnaissance and Air Force special operations units.

One survey question specially requested that they submit their definition of the term mental toughness. The results are shown below and I think you'll find them quite interesting. While reading them, ask yourself which statements align with what you already believe about mental toughness and which are new and might expand your thinking on this topic. Since these statements were made by special operators, we see the mention of combat, deaths of colleagues during combat operations, etc. I do think all of them can easily be modified so they apply to whatever environment you are operating in from a personal or professional standpoint.

Survey Results – Mental Toughness Is:

- Having unshakable confidence in your ability to achieve your goals.

- Knowing that you possess unique qualities and abilities that make you better than your opponents.

- Having an insatiable desire to succeed.

- Being resilient and able to quickly recover from adversity, disappointment, set-backs, etc.

- Thriving on the pressure of high-stakes events, including combat operations.

- Accepting that fear and anxiety are inevitable and knowing that you can overcome both.

- Able to remain fully focused on the mission.

- Remaining fully focused on the task at hand in the face of life-threatening situations.

- Being able to cope with high levels of physical and emotional pain, while still maintaining the ability to execute skills and tasks required to accomplish the mission.

- Quickly regaining psychological control following unexpected, uncontrollable events such as the death of a unit member during a combat operation.

As you can see, some common themes emerged from the survey results. Specifically, the traits of motivation, confidence, focus, composure and resilience surfaced as the essential traits for success as a special operator. I think most people intuitively know that, to perform effectively as a SEAL, men must possess a certain type of mental toughness and emotional control that enables them to cope with fear and anxiety as the levels of danger increase during combat operations. As a result of their training and mental preparation, SEALs develop an iron will that allows them this capability. They have consistently demonstrated the ability to remain composed, confident and focused during the inevitable "Fog of War" that is associated with dangerous and dynamic special operations missions. In other words, SEALs thrive in high-pressure situations and they always believe they can successfully accomplish the mission. Above all, they are mentally tough.

Traits Specific to Mental Toughness

Motivation

Any goal we set for ourselves has finality to it; there is an end-state that we are looking to achieve. Keeping this end-state in focus is in itself the motivator that will keep you moving toward it. This component of mental toughness is perhaps the most important one, because even if you possess the other four in ample amounts, they won't do you any good if you're not motivated to take action! I recommend that you ask yourself "Why am I doing this?" or "Why is it important that I achieve this goal?" This will enable you to better understand your motivations and desires, which can lead to enhanced focus and more clearly stated goals.

Confidence

Confidence is a critical ingredient to mental toughness. It enables you to know that you have the skills and knowledge to achieve the challenge or task facing you, and it also enables you to bounce back after setbacks, mistakes or poor performances. SEALs typically have an unshakeable confidence in their abilities. This comes from the fact that they have confidence in their skills and "game plan," and in their ability to execute the plan during stressful, high-pressure situations. A good way to develop this trait is through repeatedly practicing whatever skill you would like to master. If, for example, you would like to improve your public presentation skills, you would need to practice presenting to an audience repeatedly until you become very comfortable doing it. Or, if you are in a field that requires you to conduct mathematical computations very quickly, just practice it over and over until you have mastered it.

Focus

The ability to focus – to home in on what's most important at a given time – and to be able to block out everything else, is a huge factor in the development of the mental toughness that leads to an iron will.

For centuries, soldiers have talked about the "Fog of War" that occurs during battles, and how one must consciously remain focused on the mission and avoid being distracted or confused by irrelevant or insignificant issues. SEALs often refer to this as "being in the zone." It implies a state of hyper-focus on what's most important to accomplishing the mission. In everyone's life there are daily contretemps that occur without notice. It is important to be able to set those aside and not allow them to overwhelm you and divert focus from your task at hand.

Composure

In order to perform at optimal levels, you must be able to remain composed and in control during the most stressful situations. This enables you to have clarity and focus during the heat of battle and it promotes sound decision-making. Composure is all about your mind being in control of the emotions and reactions that are being produced by your brain's automatic responses to certain situations. Knowing these responses will occur enables you to cope with them by overriding your brain's signals with those being sent by your well-trained mind. Hopefully, you are starting to understand that the brain and mind are two separate things. Your body obeys the brain, but the brain obeys the mind! Prospective SEALs are constantly confronted during training with situations that require them to use their minds (mental toughness) to overcome what their brains are telling their bodies. Their brains tell BUD/S students that they are too cold during training evolutions in which they must remain in the frigid ocean for extended periods of time. Many students succumb to how their brains react and they quit the course. Those able to use their minds to remain composed and focused finish the evolution and move on to the next training task. Likewise, you will encounter possible situations where your brain will tell you that you are just too tired to finish a project, or that you simply cannot figure out a problem. It is up to your mind to remain in control and push you to stay focused until you have overcome the obstacle.

Resilience

Resilience is a critical factor of being successful in any number of professions. This trait is typically one of the most heavily discussed whenever the topic of mental toughness is being debated. Like the young men striving to gut their way through the SEAL training pipeline, you will surely face obstacles and setbacks while you work toward accomplishing your goals. Resilience is the quality that enables people to bounce back from these challenges and get back on the path to success.

Author Lars Draeger, while conducting research for his book, *Navy SEAL Training Guide: Mental Toughness*, interviewed former and active SEALs, asking them for their thoughts on what mental toughness is. See below for some of the comments gathered during the interviews.

"Mental toughness is doing whatever is necessary to accomplish the mission."

"You simply cannot be a Navy SEAL without being mentally tough. You wouldn't make it through BUD/S, and you certainly wouldn't be able to operate in combat if you weren't. SEALs must have the mental ability to block out physical pain and fear, while remaining highly focused on whatever is required to achieve victory."

"In my opinion, mental toughness is the ability to remain calm when others are overcome by fear or panic, and being able to do whatever needs to be done to win."

"Mental toughness is not letting anyone or anything break you."

"Mental toughness is not being affected by anything that might degrade your ability to achieve the mission you've been assigned. It is the ability to perform well under the worst conditions possible."

"No matter what happens, I simply refuse to lose. To me, it's really that simple. I approach anything thought to be difficult with an attitude of 'I'll do this or die trying.'"

"It means that whenever most people would make excuses why something can't be done, I focus on finding a way to get it done."

"*Mental toughness is the belief that, as long as I'm breathing and my brain is functioning, I have the ability to succeed at any given task.*"

"*I think mental toughness is a man's ability to defeat the voice in his mind that is telling him to quit.*"

"*I've seen a lot of mentally tough guys during my time in the Teams, and the common trait they possess is that they all believe that adversity brings out the best in them and that there's always a way to win.*"

"*The ability to stay focused when ordinary men would buckle under the pressure or be consumed by fear.*"

"*Being mentally tough means that you can have your arm shot off and, if necessary, pick it up with your other hand and use it as a club to kill the enemy.*"

"*My platoon did a hit on a house in Iraq, and I came face-to-face with an insurgent. For a brief moment, we looked into each other's eyes. I walked out of that house and he didn't.*"

"*I was never able to shake my fear of heights and never enjoyed jumping out of an airplane at twenty thousand feet, yet I did so hundreds of times over my twenty-year career. I simply decided that my desire to serve in the Teams was stronger than the fear I felt toward jumping. SEALs aren't immune from fear; they simply refuse to let it affect them in a negative way. That's what mental toughness means to me."*

Based on the survey results previously cited and anecdotes such as those provided in Draeger's book, other books, surveys and research studies associated with special operations forces, and the many interviews and conversations that I have engaged in with SEALs and members of other special operations units, here are my thoughts on mental toughness:

- Some people have a natural pre-disposition to mental toughness and exhibit this trait very early on in their childhood via academic, athletic and social endeavors.

- Mental toughness can be learned and developed by means of various methods and techniques.

- Mental toughness provides a psychological advantage in individuals required to continuously perform to high standards in environments associated with high levels of stress and physical danger that includes risk of death or serious injury.

- Mental toughness can be developed by people lacking physical skills. If you have a healthy brain and a high level of motivation, you can become mentally tough.

It probably goes without saying that mental toughness is an

advantageous attribute to have in any field or profession. I can't name a single aspect of my personal or professional life that hasn't benefitted from a high level of mental toughness. Your purpose for buying this book is probably connected to your desire to elevate your own mental toughness so you can achieve more in some aspect of your life. Once developed and refined, mental toughness can enable you to approach challenges and high-stress situations like SEALs approach combat operations. It can enable you to have confidence in yourself, remain focused and calm under pressure and be capable of dealing with and recover quickly from setbacks.

> *"Mastering others is strength. Mastering yourself is true power."*
>
> *~ Lao Tzu*

Decide to be Exceptional

There are people in all fields of work who are able to attain the respect and admiration of those around them. These are usually the people who have risen above their peers and have established a reputation for excellence and extraordinary achievement. Whether one is operating in the business world, academia, athletics, the military or the medical field, there are those who are considered by others to be the top performers. They are the ones that most of us would like to emulate. Most people desire to achieve excellence in some form or another; they want to be recognized as being extraordinary in some aspect of their personal or professional lives. I don't think anyone reading this book wakes up in the morning thinking, "Today, I am striving for mediocrity!" I can tell you with certainty that such thinking is never present in the SEAL community. In fact, SEALs detest mediocrity and they won't voluntarily associate with anyone who is known to accept being mediocre. That said, SEALs do realize and accept that many people do choose to be mediocre or "good enough" at various aspects of life, and they do not treat these people with disdain or disrespect.

I once had a conversation with a SEAL officer, discussing some of the people who most influenced our lives. He related that while he was a BUD/S student, one of the instructors was addressing his class on the first day of training. This instructor, who was well-known for his combat exploits in Vietnam, told the class that while BUD/S was quite difficult, several thousand men had already successfully completed the course and that there was no reason why everyone in this particular class could not do the same. He then said, "It all comes down to two choices, men, and you'll have to make one of them every single day that you are in training. You can choose to submit to your fear of failure and the physical pain which you are about to experience or you can simply remind yourself that you have a chance to join a group of exceptional men. All I can tell you is that these are the same choices I faced when I was standing where you are, and I reminded myself many times each day, especially when times got tough, that 'I choose to be an exceptional man.'

I want to take yet another opportunity to hammer home the core trait that makes SEALs what they are individually and what lies at the heart of the entire SEAL community. This trait, of course, is the *relentless pursuit of excellence* that SEALs demonstrate in all they do. Simply put – SEALs *choose* to become exceptional men. They know that becoming exceptional is not something that suddenly happens to a person, it is the result of goal setting, will, self-discipline and unwavering focus on actions that lead to excellence in everything they do.

In his book *Unleash the Warrior Within*, former SEAL, Richard "Mack" Machowicz, said this about the mental aspect of getting through BUD/S: "I had to get myself in the mindset of never giving up no matter what. A buddy of mine gave me a quote which stated, 'A man can only be beaten in two ways: if he gives up or he dies.' I had that quote in my wallet until the pencil marks rubbed off. I really lived that motto. I decided that if I am not dead, then I cannot quit." In other words, Machowicz, in his own way, had decided to become an exceptional man and had made up his mind that nothing short of dying was going to keep him from achieving his dream. This may sound a bit over-the-top or melodramatic to some… I urge you to instead view Machowicz's statement as an indicator of a person's willingness to "go all in" and hold nothing back while pursuing his or her goals, and ultimately becoming exceptional.

So, how does one go about becoming exceptional? Is there a formula for excellence that people can follow? How does a person get to the hard-to-quantify "next level" of performance and achievement? You may have hoped for an easy step-by-step formula that would guarantee success. The truth is that such a formula simply does NOT exist. If you truly wish to achieve excellence, there is only one way that will guarantee you results: you have to be willing to put in the work. You have to be willing to make it your mission to do all the things necessary to get you to that next level. In the following chapters, we will focus on some time-tested principles that can help you as you continue on your journey to personal excellence and high-achievement.

Everything you've read so far, and all that you are about to read, focuses on a simple concept that is the foundation of SEAL success: Execute all tasks with vigor and intensity; winning can be the only acceptable outcome.

Perhaps you should reflect a bit about what you want to achieve, what your goals are, perhaps even why you bought this book. Whatever it is that you desire to achieve, chances are it will require some level of focus, intensity or motivation that for various reasons, you haven't been willing or able to commit to in the past. The choices facing you are the same ones described earlier. It starts with a simple decision: you can submit to various excuses or you can *decide* that you are going to become an exceptional person.

So, what's your choice going to be?

Me?

I choose to be an exceptional man!

"Sure I am this day we are masters of our fate, that the task which has been set before us is not above our strength; that its pangs and toils are not beyond our endurance. As long as we have faith in our own cause and an unconquerable will to win, victory will not be denied us."

~ *Winston Churchill*

Defining Success

The definition of success is a personal one. It means something different to you than it does to me. It is important to define it for yourself, and to constantly refer to that definition in order to assess whether you are charting a course that will lead you to it. As you read this book, you will see the term success used quite frequently. You'll also see other terms such as *winning attitude* and *high-achievers*. So, before we get into winning and the winning mentality associated with SEALs and other high-achievers, I want to present some thoughts and perspective on success.

The definition of success really depends on where you are in life, what you've experienced (good and bad) and most importantly, where you desire to go or what you desire to accomplish. For some reading this book, success means completing the training required to become a Navy SEAL. Others may define success as graduating from college, attaining a certain income level, being promoted to a higher position at work, losing weight or increasing their level of physical fitness.

The definition of success also changes over the course of one's life. As a person enters adulthood, he or she likely has goals of getting a good education, working in a certain profession or occupation and for most, meeting that special person that they'll spend their lives with. Once all of this is accomplished, success is quickly associated with being promoted to higher paying positions, buying a home, having children, etc. All of this brings about subsequent stages of changes in what success means to people as they strive to achieve even more at work and at home.

As you age and gain experience in various aspects of life, the ways in which you define success will likely transition from professional and financial achievement to your health, spouse and children, grandchildren, your legacy, and how you will be remembered.

Winning

A common characteristic among Navy SEALs is the presence of an invincible mental attitude, which anticipates success in accomplishing any task or overcoming any challenge. The combat operations executed by these warriors are obviously quite dangerous, with the difference between success and failure often meaning whether they live or die. Thus, the exigency for success is something that resides within the very core of every SEAL.

If you ask a SEAL to share his views on winning or achieving success, he will tell you that this does not happen by chance or luck; it happens because he makes it happen. He will tell you that although an optimistic mindset is the foundation for success, focused and detailed preparation is actually the major factor behind all achievement.

Such preparation includes a combination of education and training. It includes continuous and deliberate practice of various skills in a wide range of environments or situations. In other words, being a winner is the result of continuous learning, skill development and relentless practice under realistic "game day" conditions.

One point to ponder is that even the most highly trained and competent SEAL was once an untrained civilian. He, therefore, had to learn and perfect every single skill through hard work over the course of time. This is an important point to contemplate as you decide what your goals are and how quickly you desire to achieve them. What skills or competencies are you going to need to be successful, and how long will it take you to acquire and perfect them?

I have met and worked with many members of the various U.S. special operations forces and some from the more accomplished foreign commando and counter-terrorist units. I have found that all of these individuals possess many of the same characteristics and traits, and this is likely what makes them so successful. Most are very organized in their personal and professional lives. They are always learning new skills or upgrading previously mastered ones. Most importantly they are always practicing the skills that are fundamental for executing their duties. They see mistakes or poor results as temporary setbacks that can be overcome with careful analysis and refinement of technique or execution. When confronted with challenges or obstacles, they immediately start developing plans to overcome them. SEALs don't make excuses or look to blame others for their failures or poor performances, they simply get to work figuring out what went wrong and what steps are necessary to avoid making the same mistakes again.

A story that exemplifies the "winning attitude" of a SEAL is that of Special Operator Second Class, Ryan Job. As a young high school athlete, Ryan's idea of what success would mean to him was:

1. become a Navy SEAL

2. become a fighter pilot

3. marry a beautiful woman

4. buy a big ranch where he and his wife would raise many children

Ryan started on his road to achieving his success when in 2002, after 3 years studying at the University of Washington; he decided to enlist in the Navy. Immediately after completing Navy boot-camp, Ryan reported to the BUD/S training course. After making it through the difficult training, Ryan had accomplished the first goal on his list. He had become a Navy SEAL.

In April 2006 he deployed to Ramadi, Al Anbar, Iraq with his SEAL Team. During his time in Iraq, Ryan conducted several combat operations; for one of these, he was awarded the Bronze Star with Valor for saving the lives of his fellow SEALs.

On the morning of August 2, 2006 on a roof top in Ramadi, Ryan was shot in the face by a sniper. While his SEALs worked to save his life, he regained consciousness, kept his composure, sat himself up and tried to comfort his teammates telling them he would be OK. Somehow Ryan was able to stand up and join his team as they fought their way to an awaiting helicopter. Had it not been for his training and his fellow SEALs who cared for him, Ryan probably would have died that day. The wound rendered Ryan totally blind, forcing him to medically retire from the Navy.

Before deploying to Iraq, Ryan had met a woman named Kelly, and set his sights on achieving another of his goals. Kelly's support was instrumental in helping Ryan as he endured the difficult road to recovery from his injuries. Ultimately, however, it was his drive and positive attitude that truly pulled him through the surgeries that were necessary to rebuild his face, eye socket and part of his skull. When he was informed that he would be blind for the rest of his life, Kelly recalls him saying: "Well, if I'm going to be blind, I'm going to be the best blind man there is."

Ryan and Kelly married in March of 2007, and moved to Phoenix.

With two goals achieved, and knowing that he would never be a fighter pilot, he set his sights on a new goal. He decided to shoot for achieving one of the most difficult climbs in the world, Mt. Rainier. He joined the Camp Patriot's Summit Challenge Team for the climb; and on July 2009 Job stood at the summit of Mt. Rainier having successfully achieved another goal.

His next goal was to attain his bachelor's degree in business administration. While attending classes, and at the same time working with other wounded servicemen, Ryan had to go through various surgeries to continue repairing the damage to his face. On September 24, 2009 during recovery from his last surgery, Ryan passed away suddenly. The reason for his death has been attributed to a hospital error.

Ryan had just completed his Bachelor's degree with a 4.0 GPA earlier that September. He had also landed an internship at General Dynamics, where he had been offered a full-time job. Ryan never met his daughter, who was born 6 months after his death. His winning attitude and courage after being gravely wounded serve as a superb example of the resilience and unstoppable mindset associated with Navy SEALs. Ryan Job's life can serve as an inspiration to us, as we strive to overcome the challenges and obstacles we face on a daily basis.

The achievement of 'success,' however you define it at any given point in your life, requires that you be diligent and obsessive about preparation, planning, training and constantly practicing your skills. A positive mentality and optimism will greatly impact the outcome of your endeavors. Regardless of what obstacles you may be facing, there are habits and traits that you can develop that will aid you as you face them, conquer them and continue on your journey to success.

"Happiness and freedom begin with a clear understanding of one principle: Some things are within our control, and some things are not. It is only after you have faced up to this fundamental rule and learned to distinguish between what you can and can't control that inner tranquility and outer effectiveness become possible."

~ EPICTETUS

Effective Habits

Having an ethos that rejects failure and views success as the only acceptable outcome of any mission requires all SEALs to constantly strive to develop and improve their knowledge and skills in order to uphold those beliefs. All SEALs share common traits such as physical strength, agility and endurance, and they all possess high levels of proficiency in the various skills, techniques and tactics common to those wearing the Trident. But don't for a second think that being exceptionally physically conditioned, a world class runner or Olympic level marksman is all there is to succeeding as a SEAL! What's important for you to know is that SEALs share a core suite of traits and habits that enable them to consistently perform well under very stressful conditions. Below is a list of what I feel are the most significant of these traits and habits. These are the qualities that lead to the unfailing success of individual SEALs as well as the successes demonstrated by the whole SEAL community. These are the traits that you must strive to develop in order to achieve your goal of becoming 'exceptional.'

Must Be Goal Oriented

It probably won't come as a surprise to you that SEALs are very goal-oriented individuals. It is obvious that having this trait is an essential factor in the efforts to gain entrance to and complete all phases of the training required for becoming a Navy SEAL or 'frogman'; starting with BUD/S, and following on to the continuous training that happens as they continue the journey of life as a SEAL.

Most SEALs have a very long list of personal and professional goals, which are often segmented into short-term, mid-term and long-term categories. In this book, you'll see repeated references to the competitive nature of SEALs. It is important to know that in many instances, they are competing against themselves and self-imposed goals. This is a habit that everyone who wishes to improve in their personal and professional lives can create. You can start by working on setting some simple goals that you know you can easily accomplish and then move on to more complex, longer-term ones.

Several years ago, I had a conversation with a young enlisted SEAL and he shared some of the goals he had set that were not associated with being a team guy. Included in them was being a "good husband and father," "earning a college degree," "starting a successful business" and "becoming a multi-millionaire." At the time this young man was not married. He now is and has two children – and I am sure he's well on his way to checking the box on the "good husband and father" goal. He's still serving as a SEAL, so he's not yet a millionaire, but I would bet good money that it is only a matter of time after he leaves active duty before that goal is also realized!

Everything a SEAL does is with a purpose or goal in mind – an "end state" that must be attained in order to declare "mission accomplished." The old adage, "If you fail to plan, you are planning to fail" certainly applies to the SEAL community. It is an intrinsic characteristic of all SEALs that their actions or efforts are always associated with stated, measurable goals.

Must Have Self-Discipline

A hallmark of the individual frogman is his high-level of self-discipline. This trait is probably present before he enters BUD/S, where it is greatly amplified and refined during this rite of passage. Self-discipline, in my opinion, is at the root of all that a SEAL accomplishes or fails to accomplish during his time in the teams and, really, throughout his life. It drives him to acquire additional knowledge and skills and to avoid anything that will detract from his goal of always being at the top of his game. Self-discipline is the force behind sound choices and deliberate actions that lead to positive outcomes. It allows a SEAL to withstand extreme levels of physical pain and emotional stress, and it also allows him to understand his limitations at times when it is essential to do so.

Must Have Self-Confidence

Unlike many people, SEALs do not suffer from a lack of self-confidence! To the casual observer, it might actually appear that some of these warriors are somewhat arrogant, and in some instances, they may be correct. The truth is that these warriors are simply quite comfortable in their skin – they know who they are, what they have done and what they are capable of doing. Their training and combat experiences produce a "Can Do" mentality and these men have an unshakeable confidence in their ability to seize the day and overcome anything that is thrown at them.

I want to share with you the comments made by an Army staff officer - a Major - who participated in the planning and conduct of several operations in Iraq that involved SEALs and other special operations forces. He said, "I'd never worked with SEALs before and I admit that I had some preconceived notions about their willingness to operate well with other special operations units. I expected them to come in with a "cowboy attitude" and plenty of egos, but I was wrong – dead wrong. Instead, they were eager to play a part in some rather high-profile missions, including some in which they were not the main effort. I was impressed by their competence and their quiet confidence. These guys knew they were good and they made shit happen time after time."

Throughout this book, you'll note a common theme in my writing that aligns with the Major's comments – SEALs exude an air of competence and confidence, they have a bias for action and the only thing that matters to them are results – the successful accomplishment of the mission assigned to them.

Must Be Proactive

Despite having many different types of personalities, all SEALs are in the habit of being proactive in their approach to any situation. They are all forward-looking and -thinking individuals capable of independent thought. They are self-starters with a habit of assessing what actions need to be considered or taken relative to a variety of situations or environments. They simply cannot afford to sit and wait and see what happens.

Experienced SEALs are very aware of what they can control or affect and what they cannot. Rather than waste time worrying or complaining about things that are outside of their control, they focus on what they can affect – and they plan and execute actions that are likely to lead to favorable results.

For example, while it is common knowledge that the senior enlisted SEALs, Chief Petty Officers, run the operations of a SEAL platoon, the fact is that there are two commissioned officers assigned to the unit. The senior officer is the person to whom total responsibility for all that the platoon does or fails to do is assigned. Typically, these young officers, though fully qualified as SEALs, lack the leadership experience that can only be acquired with time, and are prone to making decisions or recommendations that are less than optimal (I'm being diplomatic here!) and in some situations, can endanger the unit.

Instead of whining about young and inexperienced officers, the very best enlisted SEALs approach them as mentors and teach them how to become competent SEAL leaders. They know that an effective officer can be a huge asset to a SEAL unit and they proactively set about ensuring that their officer becomes one.

Being proactive is a trait that is expected of all SEALs and they quickly learn that nobody is going to lead them by the hand and tell them what to do. For sure, the newer and less-experienced SEALs will receive plenty of guidance and mentorship by their teammates, but once this occurs on any given topic or task, the new guys are expected to "figure it out and get it done" without further supervision.

SEALs know that it is best to control any situation which may affect them, personally or professionally. They also know that to do so, one has to project and envision that which lies unseen over the horizon, but must be planned for in advance. In other words, SEALs know that it is almost always better to be proactive than reactive. They know from experience that when forced to be reactive, they often are not in control of a situation and this can lead to undesirable situations or events, especially during combat operations.

Must Be Decisive

Decisiveness is an essential trait for a SEAL. The very nature of the type of operational missions these men are assigned requires that every member of the unit, not just officers and senior enlisted SEALs, be capable of making rapid decisions during highly fluid, extremely stressful situations. These warriors are cool under pressure, and because of their training and personality, seek to dominate any situation they may find themselves in. They are always focused on the mission and what exact sequence of events must happen in order for the mission to be deemed successful. SEALs have a bias for action because they know that, in their profession, hesitation or indecisiveness can have fatal consequences. Of course, simply making decisions is not enough. The decisions must be made using sound judgment and must produce positive results. This implies a very important point that I want to ensure readers understand: being decisive is a highly effective trait, but only when accompanied by adequate decision-making skills. It is not enough for a young SEAL officer to instinctively know he must issue direction to his platoon during a firefight; his direction and commands must be the product of a sound, albeit rapid, thought process.

Must Be Competitive

If you ever get the chance to be around a group of SEALs for any length of time, you will soon realize that they love to compete in any situation in which a winner will be declared. Every SEAL I have ever known had an intense desire to win. There are the obvious competitions, such as physical training, long-distance open-ocean swims, runs through an obstacle course or shooting evolutions that are graded for speed and accuracy.

And then there are the "informal competitions" that team guys seem to thrive on; in which just about everything is a graded event and, as such, there will be winners and losers. I've seen SEALs traveling to an off-base training event drive like moonshiners trying to evade the police to ensure their van arrives at the training site first. Taking a military aircraft to some remote location? There will be intense competition for choice spots in the aircraft where hammocks can be strung up, or where there's more room to stretch out and sleep. Once, during some time off from training in Italy, I witnessed a SEAL platoon at a beach resort rent some of those pedal-powered rafts that seat two people; and soon enough pairs of SEALs were competing in sprint races against each other and some of the tourists! Many people do not like to live and operate in this kind of continuous competition, but most SEALs do. An intense "hyper-competitiveness" permeates the entire SEAL community.

Must Be Mentally Tough

Mental toughness is a core attribute of every SEAL. Without it, it would be impossible for a man to survive BUD/S and eventually earn his Trident. Even more important, it is often a major factor in the battlefield success achieved by frogmen during extremely dangerous combat operations. As discussed earlier, there are certain factors that comprise mental toughness; and it is important that SEALs develop and maintain these in order to be effective.

Must Be Able to Overcome Adversity

SEALs have to be resilient. Whether engaged in training or actual combat operations. Challenges, conditions and situations will vary, but all are best handled by a highly trained warrior possessing an inner strength that enables him to prevail over whatever is facing him at the moment. SEALs routinely face situations in which it would seem logical for them to abort a mission or retreat in the face of unexpected enemy threats or events. During these situations, they tap the reservoir of "iron will" developed through hard training, which enables them to endure and achieve when most men would simply quit.

SEALs do encounter setbacks – things don't always go as planned, especially in combat. Plans go awry, helicopters break down or even crash, radios fail at critical moments and in some instances, their teammates are killed or wounded. Their training and inner resolve is what enables them to quickly recover during situations like these, assess the status of their plan and adapt it appropriately to accomplish the mission. SEALs actually flourish in such situations; they learn much from them and incorporate these lessons into their training and tactics.

The very nature of special warfare is such that SEAL operators must be hard men with the ability to "get the job done," no matter what it takes. For this reason, bouncing back from setbacks and losses is expected of these men and a great amount of peer pressure exists to ensure they do so. As a result of their training, SEALs expect much of themselves in this regard and they hold themselves and each other accountable to a standard in which the only acceptable outcome is success – accomplishing the mission.

This focus on results and mission accomplishment has resulted in a culture in which sympathy is not offered or expected should a SEAL fail to achieve his assigned mission. This may sound a bit cruel, but it is reflective of the harsh and unforgiving world in which these men operate. This aspect of the SEAL culture produces men who simply will not quit and there are numerous examples of them persevering when all logic tells them to quit or accept failure.

There have been cases in which SEALs have actually lost part of an arm or leg to training injuries or wounds received in combat, and over time, have returned to their units in a fully operational status. After almost 10 years of war in Iraq and Afghanistan, there are actually a few SEALs with artificial limbs operating in the Teams!

Adam Brown was a member of SEAL Team Six, the unit that killed Osama bin Laden. This unit has exceptionally high standards regarding close quarters battle shooting and, while the actual standards are classified, suffice it to say that the level of accuracy required of these men while shooting on the move in darkness and extreme conditions is so high, it almost seems unrealistic even to trained observers. Obviously, this type of shooting requires exceptional eyesight, visual acuity and hand-eye coordination. Adam lost an eye, which for most SEALs would have meant the end of their career as a shooter. Undeterred by this, he taught himself how to shoot to standard using his remaining eye. This may sound easy, but it is not. In fact, it is so difficult to do that even most of his SEAL brothers thought that Adam would not be able to regain his past proficiency in CQB shooting. But, through grit and determination, he did just that, and went on to serve in an operator role in the premier counter-terrorist unit in the U.S. military.

Adam's story takes on a new twist when he injures one of his hands and it no longer has the functional ability and dexterity to handle a pistol at the level required of a SEAL operator. This too, would normally be a crippling blow to a shooter required to maintain levels of proficiency associated with SEAL Team Six. Once again, Adam patiently and methodically trained himself to shoot to standard with his other hand and retained his status as an operator on an assault team. Sadly, Adam was killed during a combat operation in Afghanistan in 2010 and his death was a huge loss to the SEAL community. I think it appropriate to use this exceptional man as an example of resilience.

Adam's story and those of other frogmen since World War II

show that certain attitudes and traits can enhance our ability to deal with life's trials. Like SEALs, you must be capable of absorbing adversity, rolling with the punches, and rapidly rebounding. That's assuming, of course, that you aspire to high achievement and expect to encounter serious challenges and obstacles along the way!

Must Have Courage

Courage is an attribute that most people associate with Navy SEALs. Many people believe that these exceptionally tough warriors do not experience fear as a result of their training. This is not true, SEALs are not immune to fear – their brains, like those of all humans, were hard-wired through evolution to recognize dangerous or threatening situations and in turn produce fear, anxiety and other emotions or reactions that can have a negative impact on one's performance. SEALs are very effective at controlling the effects of fear, and this is what enables them to act courageously and decisively in situations that might cause other men to retreat and seek safety.

Those without combat experience are often prone to thinking that the courage displayed by servicemen is simply an act of bravery performed during a battle, and it is understandable why they'd believe this, based on what they've seen on TV and in military-themed movies. There are two forms of courage: physical courage and moral courage.

Physical courage is what most people believe it to be – the ability to overcome the natural reactions of the brain and body to dangerous or threatening situations and doing what needs to be done to accomplish the mission. It is not the absence of fear; rather it is what enables a SEAL to act with purpose and precision, despite his fear, in situations that have a high probability of him being wounded or killed.

Moral courage is often overlooked when discussing military leadership or special operators, but it is absolutely essential to the training, development and combat effectiveness of the individual SEAL and the SEAL community as a whole. Moral courage is being willing to have the courage of your convictions and standing up for what you believe is right in a specific situation, even if doing so might have negative consequences on your relationship with peers and seniors.

Both types of courage are critical to being an effective SEAL. Many readers of this book would likely believe that SEALs would need to demonstrate physical courage far more often than moral courage, but in my opinion (and that of many SEAL operators) they are wrong. The need for physical courage is obvious and it is a fact that a SEAL has to possess and demonstrate this vital attribute. But, during a SEAL's tenure in an operational unit there will be many situations that will require him to speak up and often, argue against what his senior leaders are planning to do regarding a specific training evolution or combat operation.

Any SEAL with combat experience will tell you that there are countless instances in which their leaders, the officers and senior enlisted SEALs, have had to forcefully argue with planners from higher headquarters who are attempting to assign flawed or poorly planned tactical missions to their unit. For those without military experience, let me assure you that it takes a great amount of moral courage for a relatively inexperienced, 26 year-old SEAL Lieutenant to stand tall and tactfully argue with a SEAL Captain , Marine Corps Colonel and other senior commanders and staff officers about certain aspects of a mission his platoon or task force is being assigned. But, it is often the right thing to do and in more than a few instances, it has saved lives and reduced the amount of casualties among the unit that actually has to conduct the operation.

Must Seek Knowledge

When most people hear the term "Navy SEAL," an image pops up in their mind of a powerfully built man bristling with weapons, wearing various pieces of tactical gear and looking very much like a predator ready to pounce on its prey. This is the way the media typically presents SEALs to the public and most people are heavily influenced by what they see on television and in the movies.

The truth is that, while SEALs are indeed impressive to look at when they are "dressed for work," the demands of becoming and remaining a competent frogman require continuous study and pursuit of knowledge. The very nature of the equipment and technology used in today's special operations arena presents a much more significant challenge. Therefore, a Navy SEAL must always be learning new skills or refining existing ones in order to remain a "cutting edge" special operator, otherwise he would stagnate and would eventually become a liability to his teammates.

SEALs utilize some of the most highly sophisticated equipment used by any military force in the world. Because of today's high-tech weaponry, satellite communications gear, lasers, optics and an ever-increasing amount of technical devices and tools that help them maintain an edge on the battlefield, SEALs consider it essential to constantly conduct research on the latest technologies and tools available in order to remain relevant and be able to serve optimally when needed.

The main point here is that SEALs are lifelong scholars and are continuously updating their knowledge base so it can be leveraged on the battlefield. Every SEAL that I have ever known pursued additional knowledge in some aspect of warfare that he had a particular interest in, and they did so largely during their off-duty time. Some really loved weaponry and they became experts at all aspects of combat shooting. Their interest in such things enabled them to assist in the development of new and improved sniper rifles and associated gear. A few decades ago, a small cadre of SEALs learned close quarter battle (CQB) skills and lessons from more experienced law enforcement agencies, SWAT teams of major American cities and some highly regarded foreign counter-terrorist units. They took the knowledge gained from these professional relationships and over time, developed the SEAL community's CQB capabilities into what many feel are now the very best in the world.

Other SEALs were more interested in emerging technologies and they figured out how to leverage GPS enabled devices, iPads, various open-source Google tools and commercially developed applications and technologies during the planning and conduct of combat operations. Then, there are the operators who love the combat diving aspect of being a SEAL, and they constantly search for ways to innovate and improve their equipment as well as the tactics and procedures used during such operations. Suffice it to say that when you have hundreds of men with this kind of initiative and "professional curiosity," there's little chance of the SEAL community becoming stagnant or wedded to dated or less than effective technology and tactics!

As you can see, all of the traits I have just described can be developed, learned and mastered. These "habits" or "traits" are not innate. These are the characteristics that any person with a desire to improve their personal or professional life can achieve through effort and hard work. You can also see that all of them are interconnected so that as you develop one the others are also being developed by default. These are things you do in fact have control over. Once you develop and refine these habits you will be amazed at the heightened level of efficiency you will immediately be able to display in all things. These minor changes will make you a better leader, a better manager, a better teammate, and in general, a better person!

"A man's character is his fate."

~ Heraclitus 500 A.D.

Pushing Past Limitations

As a society, we have perceived notions of what the limitations for a human being are. Proof to the contrary is evidenced by each and every Sailor who becomes a SEAL. The concept of pushing past limitations permeates the entire Navy SEAL community. In fact, the infamous BUD/S training and selection course was initially based on the assumption that men are physically capable of accomplishing at least 10 times that which is typically accepted as being the "maximum capacity" of the human body. As a result of this training, the SEAL teams are comprised of men who have proven to themselves and their teammates that they are capable of enduring what most men cannot. Much of what these warriors do on a daily basis is very dangerous and well beyond the accepted limits of the human body's capability, yet they have mastered the art of making the difficult look easy.

Obviously, the ability to push past accepted limits and norms is very important while trying to survive BUD/S and become a SEAL. I think most would agree that it is also an essential ingredient to high achievement in countless aspects of one's personal and professional life. To further illustrate the concept of "no limits thinking" and pushing past accepted boundaries, I want to introduce you to a story that doesn't get much attention these days, but is a prime example of what a motivated person can do when facing a challenge that most think is beyond attainment.

They Said It Was Impossible!

During the first several decades of the 1900s, it was generally believed among doctors, scientists and athletes that it was literally impossible for a human to run a mile in less than four minutes. Many people believed that attempting to achieve this feat would result in serious harm to the runner, and some thought it could prove fatal to anyone foolish enough to push their body to such extremes.

An English runner, Roger Bannister, had initially believed the conventional wisdom that a sub-four minute mile was impossible. Then, he broke the record for the 1500 meter run (a mile is 1600 meters) and he began to believe that he could also set a new record in the mile. His newly found belief and confidence made all of the difference; and on May 6th, 1954, Roger set a new world record, running the mile in 3 minutes and 59.4 seconds – he stunned the world by achieving the impossible!

Roger's accomplishment brought the young medical student quite a bit of fame and eventually, a Knighthood bestowed upon him by the Queen of England. His sub-four minute mile served another purpose; it showed others that it could be done. Encouraged by Roger's spectacular feat, runners around the world sharpened their focus and approach to the mile-run and here's what happened:

- 46 days later, Australia's Jim Landry broke the record again, running the mile in 3:58.

- Several weeks later Bannister and Landry both broke four minutes in the same race.

- During the next 30 years the world record for the mile has been broken 16 times.

- The record now stands at 3 minutes and 43 seconds and is held by Hicham El Guerrouj, a member of the Moroccan Olympic team.

- Since then thousands of people have run the mile in under four minutes.

- Many high school students have run sub-four minute miles.

- In 1997, Kenya's Daniel Komen ran TWO miles in LESS THAN EIGHT minutes!

Obviously, once Roger Bannister proved that the impossible was indeed possible, many others also achieved this feat, because they now knew that while difficult, running a sub-4 minute mile was indeed attainable.

Lessons Learned from Bannister's Achievement:

High-Achievers Need Support

Bannister actually had a lot of help before and during his historic run. He received a great deal of coaching on the technical aspects of world-class running and he could count on friends and family for logistical support. If you look at the video of his record-setting run, you'll see that a few teammates served as pace-setters to help him maintain the tempo required to break the four minute mark. Whatever it is that you desire to achieve, chances are that you are going to need the help of others. Aside from the obvious benefit of receiving such support, it is very beneficial to surround yourself with people who are also high-achievers that can encourage you as you push yourself toward success.

High-Achievers Must Ignore Critics

As stated earlier, the concept of a human running a sub-four minute mile had long been deemed impossible. When Bannister announced that he intended to achieve this, he was immediately met with criticism and ridicule. At the time, he was a medical student and some actually questioned his intelligence and psychological fitness for serving as a physician – they thought he was crazy! Although it took an immense amount of moral courage, he shrugged off all criticism of his pursuit of the impossible, and also weathered the fury of the British track and field establishment, which was highly critical of Bannister's training regimen. Even though what he was attempting was thought to be unattainable, these "experts" still expected him to train in a manner they thought proper. Bannister stood firm in the face of this criticism and trained as he deemed necessary. He ignored those who would tell him he was chasing an impossible dream and simply went out and proved them all wrong! The SEAL teams are full of guys who were once told by someone "you'll never make it" when they stated their desire to become a SEAL. Rather than accept the fate that others had determined for them, they ignored their critics, stepped up to the infamous BUD/S challenge and succeeded.

High-Achievers Must Push Through Pain

Most significant achievements require one to sacrifice, endure and push through challenging times. Obviously, for Bannister, his athletic feat (and the training prior to it) was accompanied by a high level of physical pain. If you've ever run at the limits of your own physical ability, you know that once you reach "full throttle" for an extended period of time your entire body feels as if it's on fire! It takes a strong will to push past this level of pain and discomfort. Bannister once said: "The man who can drive himself further once the effort gets painful is the man who will win."

In non-athletic challenges, there are often significant levels of emotional or psychological stress associated with the pursuit of high achievement. I've known people who were studying for the various tests required for gaining acceptance to law and medical schools, and others who were striving to receive a professional certification or title, such as certified public accountant, nurse practitioner, emergency medical technician, etc. These and many other challenges often require people to step outside their comfort zones and exceed limits they once thought daunting or nearly impossible. Doing so is often the difference between success and failure!

High-Achievers Ignore Existing Barriers, Boundaries and Limits

In the case of the sub-four minute mile, it was deemed physically impossible. Many excellent runners did not even attempt to break this record because they thought trying to do so was simply a painful waste of time. Bannister showed that while difficult, it was indeed possible. There are countless other examples of people doing something that was thought to be outside the limits of human endurance or physical strength.

The same is true for challenges that have nothing to do with physical or athletic ability. Most would agree that law school and medical school are very tough challenges and both are associated with high levels of attrition – many students simply can't keep up with the course load or perform well on tests. An amazing fact is that there have been more than a few people who have attended law and medical school <u>at the same time</u> and were successful at both! Tell this to most doctors and lawyers and they will likely shake their heads in disbelief, but it is true. Stories abound of immigrants coming to America with no money and an inability to speak English, yet within a few years some of them manage to become more successful in business, academics and other avenues of life than people who have lived here all of their lives and who have all of the advantages that these immigrants did not!

Whether the challenge is physical or more cerebral, the main lesson is that high-achievers approach all barriers, boundaries and limitations as being artificial and man-made. They have the ability to believe in themselves and their dreams, even when all others ridicule them or try to convince them that "it can't be done." There's an old saying that applies here: "If you can conceive it, you can achieve it!"

Self-limiting Behavior

Do you limit your ability to aspire to high-achievement or to dream lofty goals? Are you in the habit of telling yourself that something you'd like to achieve or do is too difficult or that you aren't capable of making it happen? Are you prone to making excuses for yourself whenever you begin to contemplate what you'd like to do with some aspect of your life? If you're like most people, you probably have done all of the above at some point in your life. This type of thinking is often referred to as self-limiting behavior and it is the product of a person being restricted from making progress due to their own fears, unrealistic expectations and lack of confidence in his or her ability to succeed. The effects of self-limiting behavior range from slightly diminished personal or professional achievement (and happiness!) to significant or even complete failure.

Most self-limiting behavior can be traced to a person's experiences as a child, perhaps how they were treated and raised by parents. Siblings and peers often have a major impact on how people begin to feel about themselves at a very early age, and in many instances, the attitude and level of "self-worth" developed in childhood carries on into adulthood. One thing I have noticed amongst the members of the SEAL community is that a majority of SEALs apparently were very confident and focused as children and began showing signs of high levels of self-discipline and resiliency very early on in their lives. It is common to hear stories of these warriors demonstrating a strong will and "fire in the gut" when they were growing up, as young athletes and in social or academic settings.

In other words, many of today's SEALs were once children and young adults who had a very strong belief in their ability to persevere and achieve things that many of their peers thought too difficult. If you were able to speak with the high school and college classmates, teachers and coaches of men currently serving in the SEAL teams, you'd invariably come away with the impression that these people were not surprised to see these men volunteer for and complete the training required to become a frogman. Adjectives such as "dedicated, focused, strong-willed and confident" would inevitably surface in these conversations.

Traits of High-Achievers

If you were able to study the psychological profiles of people who have achieved great success, you'll easily see patterns of thought and behavior that emerge as common denominators amongst them. Whether they are athletes, scholars, scientists, inventors or entrepreneurs, they have all demonstrated the ability to push through barriers and limitations that others deemed insurmountable. In some instances, such as Roger Bannister's record-breaking run, they achieved things that rational people truly believed were beyond the reach of human beings. Many of these high-achievers were of average intelligence and more than a few had performed badly in traditional academic environments. Many had little or no formal training in areas in which they later became quite successful. In some instances, they were deemed "losers" by their families and friends. Obviously they weren't losers – far from it!

Here's something else they were not – conformists. Instead of conforming to the conventional wisdom and limitations that others allowed themselves to be constrained by, these people simply went about achieving that which the "experts" would not even attempt to do! Unfortunately, most people do conform to the limitations and boundaries created by others. They don't realize that they are allowing the thoughts and beliefs of others to limit their thinking, and in the process, their level of success and achievement in many aspects of life!

A perfect example of how sheer determination can help a person push through barriers that would be insurmountable without this sort of mental toughness is the story of Navy SEAL Lieutenant Jason "Jay" Redman. In September of 2007 while leading a mission to capture an Al Qaeda commander, Lieutenant Redman's assault team came under heavy machine gun and small arms fire and he was severely wounded in the ensuing firefight. Lieutenant Redman was hit by multiple bullets in the face and arm. Redman's treatment has included about 1,200 stitches, 200 staples, 15 skin grafts and a tracheotomy that he wore for seven months.

While recovering at Bethesda Naval Medical Center, Lieutenant Redman hung a bright orange sign on his door, which became a statement for wounded warriors everywhere. Pictures of the sign went viral on Facebook and other social media platforms, and it was the subject of many television and cable news shows. The sign was framed and it now hangs in the Wounded Ward at the Bethesda Medical Center.

This is what his sign said:

"Attention – To all those who enter here.

If you are coming into this room with sorrow or to feel sorry for my wounds, go elsewhere.

The wounds I received, I got in a job I love, doing it for people

I love, supporting the freedom of a country I deeply love. I am incredibly tough and will make a full recovery.

What is full? That is the absolute utmost physically my body has the ability to recover. Then I will push that about 20% further through sheer mental tenacity. This room you are about to enter is a room of fun, optimism, and intense rapid regrowth. If you are not prepared for that

Go Elsewhere.

From: The Management"

After 37 surgeries, Lieutenant Redman continues to use his positive attitude to motivate others and to support various charities and causes associated with America's wounded warriors. In the summer of 2010, he joined three other wounded service members and climbed to the summit of Mount Rainier, as a testament to wounded warriors, and to show others that there is no obstacle that cannot be overcome if you have the drive, the determination, and the tenacity to rise above. Lieutenant Redmond is also an author and he has started a career as a motivational speaker.

Thinking Without Limits

If you are over 30 years of age, chances are that you know someone, personally or professionally, who has achieved things and attained levels of success that you have not. In many instances, you know for a fact that this person is not smarter than you, nor does he or she work any harder than you do. In many cases, this person does not have the same educational background or experience level that you possess. Yet, this person has somehow achieved things that you would like to achieve, but have not. While each situation is unique, I think it is safe to say that at some point in time, the person who has outperformed you demonstrated the one trait that is critical to success in any endeavor – self-confidence. This is the trait that enabled this person to believe that his or her goal was achievable, even if others believed it was not. Rather than focus on how hard it was going to be to attain the goal, or how much sacrifice was going to be required to succeed, he or she simply took action and started the journey to accomplishing the mission. In other words, while you were engaging in self-limiting behavior (perhaps without even knowing it), this person was engaged in thinking without limits. And the rest, as they say, is history! Do not despair, however, because the good news is that thinking without limits does not cost money and you can start doing it right now! To help you do so, I will share some additional examples of people who achieved the "impossible" by thinking without limits.

Even if you are not a fan of basketball, you likely know that in order to play this sport professionally, one has to be tall, much taller in fact, than the average human. It is a fact that the average height of the members of all the teams in the National Basketball Association is 6'7" and many of them weigh nearly 300 lbs. These guys are literally giants among men in a physical sense! Most people would readily accept that men under 6 feet tall would have little chance of obtaining a spot on an NBA team roster, yet it has been done! In a sport dominated by giants, players like Spud Webb (5'7"), Muggsy Bogues (5'3") and Earl Boykins (5'5") not only competed, but they performed at a higher level of success than many of their taller opponents! While these individuals are extreme examples of unusually short men making the grade as professional basketball players, there have been many players under 6' tall that have prospered in the NBA. How is this possible? The answer is obvious – all along they were thinking without limits!

Here's a story associated with thinking without limits that you may not have heard before. In 1939, a University of California–Berkeley graduate student named George Dantzig was 15 minutes late to one of his advanced mathematics classes. Prior to his arrival, the professor had written two famous examples of "unsolvable" statistics problems on the blackboard and briefly discussed them with the students. When he sat down, Dantzig saw the problems on the blackboard, assumed they were homework assignments and wrote them down. Later in the week, he handed in his homework to the professor and went about his daily routine.

A few days later, Dantzig was awakened by his professor banging on his door at 6am. When he opened his door he heard the professor exclaim, "You did it! You solved the problems that nobody else could solve!" George Dantzig had indeed solved two statistical problems that had been deemed "unsolvable" by the world-wide science and mathematics communities for many decades. When asked about the problems, Dantzig admitted that they had seemed "more difficult than the typical homework assigned by the professor," but he simply kept working on them for a few days until he arrived at a solution for both of them. This is an instance in which a person wasn't even aware that what he was attempting to do was "impossible." Because Dantzig didn't know these problems "couldn't be solved" he approached them with confidence, knowing that his professor's homework assignments, while often difficult, were always solvable. Dantzig solved the problems because he didn't know he couldn't! This is a great example of thinking without limits and how much a person can accomplish if he or she isn't constrained by boundaries, limits or "impossible" situations.

Another example of what thinking-without-limits can do for a person is the story of distance-swimmer Diana Nyad. When she was 29 years old, she set a goal for herself to swim from Cuba to Key West, Florida. Her first attempt at this feat, in 1978, failed as did three subsequent attempts over the next 30 years. Finally, on September 2, 2013, at the age of 64, after swimming more than 100 miles in shark-infested waters, Diana achieved her long time goal. After her 53-hour ordeal was over, she told reporters, "I got three messages. One is we should never, ever give up. Two is you never are too old to chase your dreams. Three is it looks like a solitary sport, but it's a team effort."

Yet one more story that shows what not limiting our thinking can do is one that happened some years ago. A highly regarded SEAL lieutenant was injured in a training accident and, as a result, lost the lower portion of one of his legs, starting about 3" below the knee joint. At the time (mid-1980s), medical science and prosthetic limbs were not as advanced as they are today, and this young officer's injury was considered by doctors and senior SEAL leaders to be one that rendered him incapable of continued service as a SEAL. When the mention of being medically retired began surfacing in conversations with doctors and his SEAL leaders, this officer politely and defiantly declared that he intended to recover from his injury and return to his unit as an operator. He assured anyone who'd listen to him that all he wanted was the opportunity to recover from the injury and regain the ability to meet the physical standards of being a SEAL.

I don't think anyone involved in this situation doubted the young officer's desire to return to his unit. But, I'd say that nearly all of them simply couldn't fathom a man missing the lower part of his leg, even one who'd already served as a fully qualified SEAL, would be able to meet the physical standards associated with being an operator. To make a long story short, this officer not only made it back to his unit as a fully capable SEAL, but he went on to become a highly accomplished senior officer and commander of a Naval Special Warfare Group.

There are countless stories of high-achievers, like the SEAL officer mentioned above, who have achieved great things mainly because they believed they could. These people know that within each person - including you - is a reservoir of untapped potential and capability that is waiting to be used. All that is needed to unleash this "secret weapon" is the decision to use it. Once you decide that it is time to stretch yourself and go past boundaries and limits that previously stopped you, there's literally no limit to what you can achieve!

What's Your Four-Minute Mile?

Is there something you want to achieve or do that everyone else thinks is impossible? Something that perhaps even you think is unattainable? Maybe you've actually started pursuing this goal and gave up when faced with difficulties? Perhaps you made an attempt and failed the test, examination or whatever it was that was associated with deciding success or failure? Your four-minute mile might be something that many others have accomplished, it just seems unattainable or "too hard" for you.

All of these are just limitations that your mind has created because of its incapability to believe in your ability to accomplish something. In order to succeed, you must start believing you can win – it is really as simple as that. Whatever it is that you want to achieve, the first step to achieving it is to convince yourself that while it may be difficult, you can in fact do it. It is this self-belief that enables you to ignore the critics and do whatever it takes to reach your goal.

"They can because they think they can."

~ Virgil, 30 B.C.

Four Levels of Competence

As you begin to set your goals and develop a plan to reach them, I am sure that most readers of this book will need to learn new skills or greatly enhance existing ones in order to attain their goal. So, I thought it appropriate to present some information and perspective on the topics of learning and competence. Most of this information is common sense, but for most readers, it will be the first time they've ever seen it written down in one place. I think that you'll find it interesting and that it can help you achieve whatever it is that you aspire to.

The concept that learning is comprised of four levels has been around at least since the 1970s. Some attribute it to the famous psychologist Abraham Maslow, while others believe that it was developed by those working in the field of clinical psychology and disciplines related to human behavior and training. Over time, this concept has become known as the "Four Levels of Competence" and it has direct application to the training and development of Navy SEALs, and most likely, the career path or life goals that you are pursuing.

This concept suggests that individuals are typically unaware of what they don't know (or how little they know about a specific topic), which makes them unconscious of their incompetence. Upon recognizing their incompetence, they decide to focus on acquiring the knowledge and skills necessary to become competent. Having reached that point, they are conscious of the fact that they have become competent and with continued practice and refinement, they can eventually perform the newly acquired skills "automatically," without the need for deliberate thought as they execute or perform them.

I think it is safe to say that as you read this chapter, you will easily understand the elements of the "Four Levels of Competence" and will quickly see how you've been through the four stages many times during your life. The concept has undeniable merit and utility, whether it is applied to the training and development of Navy SEALs or your own plan for self-improvement or attainment of your goals.

As I walk you through the four levels and how they apply to prospective and even relatively inexperienced SEALs, I will use weapons handling and close quarter battle (CQB) shooting skills as a vehicle for discussion. I could use any number of SEAL related skills such as advanced free-fall parachuting techniques, the operation of sophisticated technical devices, the employment of swimmer delivery vehicles operating from the deck of a submerged submarine or even the planning and conduct of combat operations. SEALs have to be competent in a wide range of skills – too many to list in this chapter. So, for the sake of simplicity, I'll use CQB and the development of BUD/S graduates into fully qualified SEAL shooters to explain the Four Stages of Competence concept.

THE FOUR LEVELS
OF COMPETENCE

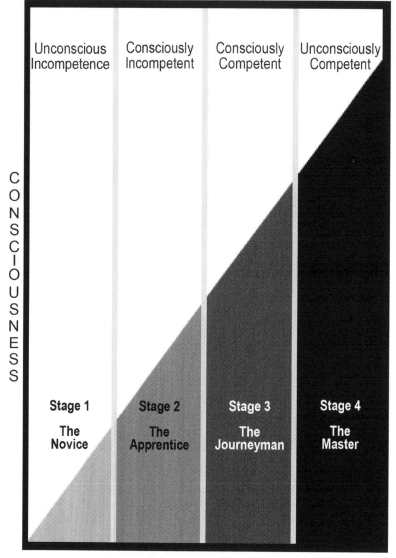

© Iron Will/Jack Calico

Level 1: Unconscious Incompetence

When a BUD/S class starts training, the students all fall into the unconsciously incompetent (UI) group. Most, if not all, of the students have watched countless SEAL videos and read many books related to the SEAL community. Many have actually been able to interact with current and former SEALs prior to arriving at BUD/S. As a result, most of them actually think they know what being a SEAL is all about. The truth is that unless they progress past Hell Week and start learning the nuances of being a combat diver, they won't even begin to get a sense that they "don't know what they don't know" in relation to serving as a frogman. Even then, they won't have a true appreciation for what they will learn throughout the remainder of BUD/S and during the follow-on SEAL Qualification Training (SQT). Examples of unconscious incompetence can be found everywhere amongst BUD/S students. As previously stated, they have no idea of what is involved in operating some of the sophisticated dive gear, weapons, communications and other highly technical equipment, much less how to orchestrate it all into an effective plan of attack. Another example of their unconscious incompetence is that even though during BUD/S and some stages of SQT they are exposed to the fundamentals of military small arms and the basics of CQB tactics and techniques, they still have yet to be exposed to the final stages of training and evaluation on this critical skill. Once they are, they quickly move from the unconscious incompetence level into the next stage of learning –

conscious incompetence!

Level 2: Consciously Incompetent

At some point during SQT, the students (they still are not SEALs) realize that they have been unaware of the many primary and secondary skills that are associated with becoming a fully qualified "shooter." Now conscious of their incompetence, they begin to understand that while they have learned how to operate a rifle and handgun, they aren't even close to meeting the minimum standards that they will have to meet in order to become fully qualified SEAL shooters. Even after graduation from SQT and reporting into their first operational unit, these newly designated SEALS will remain in the consciously incompetent group for quite some time as they are exposed to additional training and execute countless CQB drills and graded live-fire exercises. Aware that they still lack a high-level of competence in some aspects of shooting, they willingly seek help in acquiring mastery of these skills. In the SEAL teams, new operators become highly motivated "students of the gun" and become determined to learn and do whatever is necessary to become qualified and accepted by their more experienced teammates as being "good to go" regarding CQB operations.

Level 3: Consciously Competent

As they are exposed to the proper training and continuous

practice, the consciously incompetent SEALs begin to quickly develop competence. Aided by the fact that they are receiving what some feel is the very best CQB training in the world and are being coached (often on an individual basis) by highly competent instructors, these new operators begin to demonstrate their ability to "shoot to standard" under a variety of conditions and during exercises and scenarios of ever increasing difficulty. What once seemed difficult or perhaps even impossible in terms of the speed and accuracy they were expected to demonstrate now seems much more attainable. Their movement through the dark hallways and rooms of the shooting houses becomes more fluid and efficient. Reloading and clearing of weapon malfunctions becomes almost effortless, as does the transition from rifle to pistol when the situation requires it. Decisions regarding "friend or foe" and "shoot/don't shoot" are made much more quickly; and they begin to develop as solid members of an assault team. That said, despite this newly acquired competence, they are still consciously thinking about almost all of the skills they are performing. At this point, every decision and action is the result of an intricate thought process and these men have not yet reached a reflex response level that many SEALs refer to as "being in the zone." They are still not ready for real-world CQB operations that require split second, reflex-driven decisions. Only with continued practice under realistic and demanding conditions can they cross into the unconsciously competent stage.

Level 4: Unconsciously Competent

The final and ultimate stage of competence implies that the shooters have, after performing thousands of repetitions of various CQB skills and techniques, literally programmed their minds and bodies to react and execute without any perceivable thought or deliberation. At this level of competence, the shooters can move rapidly through a building, clearing it of enemy forces (killing them). When the operation is completed, they often realize that they changed the magazines in their weapon once or twice during the assault, yet they have little or no memory of doing so. They are now able to perform flawlessly during very stressful and dynamic situations because their extensive training overrides their conscious thought processes. Individually, and as a team, they can now execute at the level of speed, precision and accuracy that is required during missions that involve CQB, more specialized operations such as hostage rescue missions (where the presence of innocent civilians greatly complicates things) and high-profile operations such as the one in which operators from SEAL Team Six killed the notorious Al Qaeda leader, Osama bin Laden.

An example of this phenomenon of Unconscious Competence can best be described by the account of how Navy SEAL Senior Chief Matt Dale was able to survive an "arms-length" CQB encounter during a direct-action mission in Iraq. This anecdote is taken from the book *The Sheriff of Ramadi* by retired Navy SEAL Captain Dick Couch:

"On this day Senior Chief Dale needed all of that and more.

The three insurgents focused their attention and guns on Matt Dale. One of their initial bursts took off part of his thumb and knocked away his rifle. As he had done so often in simulation, Chief Dale reached for the pistol on his hip, a Sig Saur 9mm, and brought the weapon level. Then he began to shoot: sight picture and squeeze, sight picture and squeeze, sight picture and squeeze. While Dale was shooting them, they were shooting him. The Senior Chief was hit an astonishing twenty-seven times. Eleven of those rounds were stopped by his body armor. Sixteen of those rounds went through him. "It was easier to say where I wasn't hit than where I was hit". But when it was over, three insurgents lay dead and Matt Dale was still standing.

"I didn't have time to think about it," Chief Dale told me, "My primary (weapon) was gone before I got a round off. The rest was instinct and training. I knew I had to get my pistol and there it was, in my hand and I was shooting." I asked him what he was thinking - was feeling. "Pure anger," he said. "I don't remember much other than I was incredibly pissed off - that they had shot away my rifle and that they were shooting at me. I guess I was able to focus all my anger on the insurgents and stay in the fight. I didn't stop shooting until the slide locked and they were all down."

As an aside, I believe that Captain Couch's many books on the SEAL community and other special operations forces are some of the very best that have been written to date. If you're seeking knowledge and perspective on these topics, you won't go wrong buying any book authored by this highly-respected frogman.

Your Journey through the Four Levels of Competence

Whatever your goals are, you will almost certainly progress through the Four Levels of Competence as you attempt to achieve them. This is especially true if your goals are exceptionally challenging or if they are associated with tasks, skills or topics in which you have little or no experience. Remember, all Navy SEALs, including those on the bin Laden mission, were once at the Unconscious Incompetence level in just about every skill associated with being part of that operation. At one point in their career, none of them knew how to handle weapons with the level of competence associated with serving as a shooter in SEAL Team Six. Likewise, as new SEALs, very few of them had any awareness that some of the specialized equipment and technology used in the execution of that operation even existed! The point is that all high-achievers, including those who have already achieved what you may aspire to accomplish, were once beginners and didn't possess the knowledge, skills and competence required to achieve great things.

Upon achieving competence, you will soon realize that it doesn't end there. You will inevitably see that all the hard work you did to become competent in a skill will all be in vain if you don't do the work to remain competent. Remember that most professional arenas are very dynamic and technologies are constantly changing and being upgraded. So whether you are trying to learn a new skill for work, attain a weight-loss goal, become a better salesman or learn a new medical technique, it is almost a given that if you stop practicing what you've mastered and trying to constantly improve upon it, you will become stagnant, irrelevant and ultimately once again incompetent.

"Carpe diem! Rejoice while you are alive; enjoy the day; live life to the fullest; make the most of what you have. It is later than you think."

~ Horace

Earn Your Trident Every Day

The SEAL Ethos states in part, "By wearing the Trident I accept the responsibility of my chosen profession and way of life. It is a privilege that I must earn every day." These words allude to the philosophy that permeates the SEAL community that no SEAL can ever rest on his laurels or be satisfied with his current level of knowledge, skill, physical fitness or any other aspect of serving as a frogman. This philosophy has been summarized in a statement known to all SEALs - *Earn Your Trident Every Day!*

This statement, as powerful as it is brief, reminds every SEAL that there is always something that he can do to improve, and that in the SEAL community, continuous improvement is something that is expected. It is simply what SEALs do, and it applies to everything they do, for as long as they live.

"Earn Your Trident Everyday" means that every day one must

push past the limits of yesterday's performance or achievements. It means turning weaknesses into strengths and strengths into superior capabilities. It implies that perfection is the goal; and that at the end of every day every SEAL must be able to reflect that he did everything possible to improve himself and, by extension, his beloved SEAL brotherhood.

One would think that by the time a newly-designated SEAL reports into his first operational unit his teammates would welcome him with open arms and invite him to sit down in the team room to have a beer with his peers. If you ever get the chance to speak with a SEAL about this topic, you'll quickly learn that things don't exactly happen this way! By the time a man has completed the long training pipeline required to earn the Trident, it is only natural that he might feel proud of his achievement and perhaps even start thinking he has finally cleared the final hurdle to full acceptance into the SEAL teams. In the rare event that a new frogman start thinking he's made the grade and can relax a bit, his teammates are waiting with their own version of a welcoming committee!

The traditional "welcome aboard" reception that awaits new SEALs has evolved over time as a way of impressing upon new SEALs that even though they now wear the Trident, they are still unproven and unseasoned new guys, that they have much to prove to their teammates before they will be fully accepted as operators in the fullest sense. Enlisted or officer, every new SEAL will once again face a series of "evolutions," except that unlike those in BUD/S and SQT, these evolutions and tests are, for the most part, unscripted and unscheduled, with the sole purpose of humbling the incoming rookies and reminding them that their journey as SEALs has just begun; that they indeed must earn their Trident every day!

Selection Is Continuous

In a previous chapter you learned the differences between military courses that are designed for training versus selection purposes. Every major special operations unit in the world has some form of selection process that serves as the gate through which one must pass in order to become a member of the unit. As in the SEAL teams, members of these units soon realize that the hard work and evaluation process doesn't end with passing the selection process. In other words, if getting into the unit was hard, remaining in it is even harder!

In a SEAL unit, whenever an exceptionally arduous training evolution is about to be initiated, it is not uncommon to hear SEALs joke amongst themselves with the phrase, "Selection is continuous." This phrase is also used to project the feeling that higher headquarters has made a poor decision when directing the activities of the various platoons within a SEAL team. The term is used in many situations to express various sentiments such as anger, humor and disgust. I've often heard this saying used by members of other SOF units, and I suspect it was coined by members of our legendary and highly-respected British peers – the Special Air Service.

Its use to describe emotions or feelings aside, the concept of "Selection is Continuous" is a very real one within the SEAL community. As stated earlier, once they arrive at their first operational unit, newly-designated SEALs quickly discover that they are at the bottom of the depth chart, so to speak, and are very much considered untested newbies by the veteran frogmen. Over time and with solid performance, these rookie SEALs or FNG's, as they are often affectionately referred to, will become fully accepted by their brother SEALs, but one thing will not change – the constant presence of testing and evaluation of the individual SEAL operator, in both formal and informal ways. If you are to truly understand how SEALs think and approach life, you must carefully study and reflect upon what you are about to read in this chapter.

Why SEALs Continuously Test Themselves

The journey to becoming a SEAL is a long and difficult one. So difficult, that 75% of those who enter the training pipeline fail to successfully complete it. It is obvious that every man that begins the training is aware of the fact that the odds of success are stacked against him, and that the training itself is often quite brutal from a physical endurance perspective. Why then, do so many young men subject themselves to such agony?

One psychologist working within the Naval Special Warfare

community told me, "The men who desire to become SEALs have an innate thirst for high-achievement. They want to separate themselves from other men by way of their accomplishments and by achieving things that most cannot." He went on to say that most high-achievers in sports, the business world, science and academia, automobile racing, etc., share a common need for excitement and the surge of adrenaline that is associated with performing at the outer limits of whatever it is they are doing at the time. Studies have shown that the levels of adrenaline, endorphins and other "feel good" substances produced by the human body are as comparable in stock traders on the floor of the New York Stock Exchange, doctors performing lengthy surgical procedures and salesmen pitching their product or services to high-level executives, as they are to those found in extreme athletes or military personnel engaging in high-risk operations. In other words, SEALs, like most high-achievers, crave the excitement associated with taking on significant challenges, including ones that involve the risk of death or serious injury.

"We want to be in a situation under maximum pressure,
maximum intensity, and maximum danger. When it is
shared with others, it provides a bond which is stronger than
any tie that can exist."

- SEAL Team Six Officer

"It's a mindset that is prevalent in the SEAL community," said the psychologist, who has worked with SEALs for almost a decade. "What you have is a bunch of highly trained, very capable men who don't seem happy unless they are being measured or evaluated in some way, by others or by themselves. The higher the standard they are being judged against, the better." He went on to say, "Most outsiders would think that once a man becomes a SEAL and joins a team, that he's able to relax a bit and enjoy his newly-acquired status as a member of an elite group of warriors. That's not what happens. Instead, newly minted SEALs discover that while they are now wearing the same highly coveted Trident insignia as their more seasoned teammates, they are being looked at as unknown quantities and must prove themselves worthy of being trusted with the lives of those who have been operating as SEALs for a decade or longer. It is part of what makes the SEALs unique; the test is never over and you have to earn your Trident every day."

What Motivates SEALs

Why do the vast majority of SEALs continuously seek to push themselves beyond established limits, when most people are content to settle for far less demanding lives? Here's the psychologist's response, "It's the innate need for achievement that is shared by most SEALs, the accomplishment of goals, specifically, exceptionally demanding goals that are typically seen as unattainable by most people. Coming in as a close second motivator is the competitive factor. SEALs love to win and the only way one is able to win is to compete. The competition can be against fellow SEALs, or anyone for that matter; but I can assure you that if a SEAL is in a room with at least one other person, he's competing in some way against that person, even if that person isn't aware of it!"

Studies of top level achievers in various professions and competitive environments such as world-class sports depict the same need for success, attainment of lofty goals, and of a sheer love of competing against someone or some type of measurable standard. For SEALs, whether the goal is to become the best sniper in his unit or finishing a night land navigation exercise in record time, achieving success with a competitive edge is the sought after prize. They enjoy knowing that they are among the few who have dreamed of living the life of a SEAL, and actually achieved the dream.

"It's a sense of identity," said one SEAL. "The SEAL community is very small. There aren't many men who have the ability to continuously train and push themselves to the degree that we do. Professional athletes earn a lot of money and fame, but to be honest, I'd rather have the feeling of knowing that I'm living a life (as a SEAL) that very few men can live."

The Adrenaline Factor

The adrenaline factor likely plays a role in explaining why SEALs constantly seek to test themselves against the outer limits of various physical and mental skills and challenges. An "adrenaline surge" courses through the body when the adrenal glands are stimulated through heightened activity or other stressors. This surge is part of the release of a number of hormones, including adrenaline. For many SEALs, this feeling is one that they cannot get enough of.

"A lot of SEALs openly admit that they are seeking that rush," says a Navy psychologist who has worked with the SEAL community. "They're looking for those sensations they get from putting their life on the line during dangerous training evolutions or even actual combat operations. For many, it is a feeling that they cannot get elsewhere – a feeling of acute awareness and crystal-clear focus, of knowing they are exceeding expectations. They either succeed and live – or they die. It's very much a primitive thing, but SEALs love it and they seek it out at every opportunity."

Pushing the Limits

Why do the vast majority of SEALs feel a need to push themselves to the next level, closer to the edge of established barriers and limits? Why is it that their last accomplishment is never good enough?

"SEALs say that it simply isn't rewarding to repeatedly accomplish the same goals or conquer the same challenges, even if they are quite significant and perhaps even dangerous," says the psychologist. "Performing the same activities and doing well at them simply doesn't bring the same amount of excitement as it did the first time, so they want to push themselves even farther and go for the next big goal."

He went on to say, "It is a mindset that men who are drawn to the SEAL community are risk takers. This trait, combined with a love of pushing themselves past previous physical and mental limits, is what makes SEALs unique as individuals. When you have a few hundred of them assigned to the same SEAL team, what you get is a group of high-achievers who are constantly competing against each other. The result is what you'd expect − a high-testosterone ultra-competitive group of winners who revel in testing themselves against any and all opponents and challenges."

All of the above is reflective of one of the classic SEAL sayings:

"The Only Easy Day Was Yesterday!"

SEAL Missions

Now that you have an enhanced level of awareness of the difficult training that becoming a Navy SEAL entails, I thought it would be beneficial to introduce you to some of the missions and associated physical tasks they routinely perform during training and combat operations. This information in itself is quite interesting, and if you don't know much about what SEALs do, you're probably going to be somewhat amazed by the level of physical endurance and stamina required of these warriors.

While the physical aspect of serving as a SEAL is indeed impressive, I want to cause you to reflect more deeply into the iron will, mental approach, resolve and sheer tenacity required of these men while they conduct these operations on a continual basis. When you look at these missions and physical tasks, imagine how much self-discipline and mental toughness is required to keep a man moving forward and focused on accomplishing the assigned mission; all the while remembering that during many of these operations, SEALs are facing enemy forces that are trying to kill them!

In war, competing with the enemy is not the goal. Seeking merely to compete with determined and in some cases, fanatical men, trying to kill you is a recipe for disaster. The goal is not to compete, but to dominate, specifically, domination to the point of completely overwhelming the enemy and killing him before he has the chance to do the same to you.

During an interview on a nationally-televised talk-show, the host of the show was discussing with a Navy SEAL the various countries he had been sent to during his career. She was quite impressed that this SEAL had been to so many different places around the world, however, she was completely missing the main reason behind his travels. This brief exchange, which happened during the interview, brought to the show's host an immediate focus on the reality of what SEALs do, and I thought it was worth sharing.

> *Interviewer: "Did you have to learn several languages?"*
> *Navy SEAL: "No, ma'am, we don't go there to talk."*
> *Interviewer: "Oh...I see...ok."*

It is important that you understand that <u>Navy SEALs exist for one purpose</u> - as implied by the comment made by the SEAL during that interview – <u>to kill the enemies of the Unites States</u>.

Sound cruel or barbaric?

Perhaps... but it is also reality. The cold, hard truth is that the battlefield is often associated with conditions and actions that most people would consider savage or uncivilized. We're not talking about sports or business here – we're talking about the stark reality of the "kill or be killed" situations that SEALs have been faced with since World War II. In such situations, competing is simply not good enough. Those who walk onto the battlefield to compete typically end up dying; however those who came to dominate are the ones who walk off the battlefield, often bloodied and battered, but alive. The highly competitive nature of SEALs is mentioned in various parts of this book, and I want to make sure that you understand that when I say that SEALs are competitive it means that they have a very real drive for not simply winning, but dominating!

One thing that makes SEALs unique is that this attitude of "domination versus competition" is infused into the entire culture of the Teams. Everyone associated with the SEAL community, be they SEALs or support personnel, operates with a mindset of "maxing out" and achieving excellence in everything that they do. This mindset stems from the early lessons all SEALs learn at BUD/S, where students are constantly reminded that *"It Pays to be A Winner!"* This mindset is developed through various forms of competition and brutally difficult training, and it is intended to transform the mentality of those who will go on to serve as SEALs from that of simply being a competitor trying to win an event, to a warrior who ruthlessly and relentlessly seeks to dominate the enemy and any other factor that might threaten the successful accomplishment of the mission.

I know that the vast majority of people reading this book will have no association with the military, and therefore have no chance of actually going to war in the literal sense. But, as stated previously, the mission of the book is to help you understand the mindset and invincible mentality that infuse the iron will of Navy SEALs. To do so, one must always remember why the SEAL teams exist and why the training to become a SEAL is so difficult.

Much of the information contained in this chapter was extracted from a research study conducted by the Naval Special Warfare Command. The purpose of the study was to identify physically demanding missions and mission segments performed during SEAL operations and to rank them according to their importance to mission success. The ultimate objective was to identify the abilities that contribute to success as a SEAL operator. Not surprisingly, some personality traits and intellectual skills, such as problem solving, assertiveness and the ability to work effectively as a member of a Team, emerged during interviews of several dozen highly experienced SEALs as being even more important to the probable success of a SEAL operator than many physical attributes and abilities.

The study results imply a need for high-levels of mental toughness in SEALs, which, of course, aligns with the main purpose of this book

– learning about the mindset common to all SEALs.

Survey Results

Interviews of the veteran SEALs revealed 23 traits and abilities that were felt to be the primary factors associated with successful SEAL operators. The chart below depicts these traits and abilities. It shows the weighting or *mean score* for each, which will enable readers to get a sense of how those being questioned felt about them. I've also included the definitions used for each of the traits and abilities which were used during the interviews to ensure that all participants in the study were basing their opinions from common definitions and interpretations.

I think it is important to review the study results from the perspective of this book. Note how many of the most important traits and skills, as defined by highly experienced SEALs, are mental versus physical. If you review, for example, the definitions for *teamwork* and *problem solving*, you'll quickly realize that there are many, perhaps dozens of associated traits and skills implied in each, almost all of which are mental attributes.

Rank order and mean overall score of abilities contributing to success as a SEAL.

NAVY SEAL TRAITS & ABILITIES

RANK	TRAIT or ABILITY	MEAN-SCORE
MORE IMPORTANT		
1	Teamwork	4.68
2	Stamina	6.36
3	Problem Solving	6.99
4	Reaction Time	8.33
5	Assertiveness	9.97
6	Strength	10.68
7	Night Vision	11.49
8	Memorization	12.47
IMPORTANT		
1	Peripheral Vision	13.96
2	Depth Perception	14.06
3	Manual Dexterity	14.10
4	Oral Comprehension	14.16
5	Far Vision	14.42
6	Near Vision	15.38
7	Arm-Hand Steadiness	15.64
8	Oral Expression	15.78
9	Speed of Limb Movement	16.59
10	Finger Dexterity	17.50
11	Color Discrimination	18.58
12	Written Comprehension	19.05
13	Control Precision	20.77
14	Math Reasoning	21.37
15	Written Expression	21.71

- Teamwork: The ability to work with others as part of a team, to anticipate what others want or need, and to cooperate.

- Stamina: The ability to maintain physical activity over prolonged periods of time.

- Problem Solving: The ability to perceive small details and "size-up" situations quickly and accurately, and then respond with an appropriate course of action.

- Reaction Time: The speed with which a single motor response can be made following the onset of a single stimulus.

- Assertiveness: The ability to bring a problem or important information to the attention of another crew member in a timely fashion.

- Strength: The amount of muscular force that can be exerted.

- Night Vision: The ability to see under low light conditions.

  Memorization: The ability to remember information, such as words, numbers, pictures, and procedures.

- Peripheral Vision: The ability to perceive objects or movement towards the edges of the visual field.

- Depth Perception: The ability to distinguish which of several objects is nearer or more distant, or to judge the distance to an object.

- Manual Dexterity: The ability to make skillful, coordinated movements of a hand together with its arm--may involve equipment, but not equipment controls.

- Oral Comprehension: The ability to understand spoken English words or sentences.

- Far Vision: The ability to see distant environmental surroundings.

- Near Vision: The ability to see close environmental surroundings.

- Arm-Hand Steadiness: The ability to make precise, steady arm-hand positioning movements

- Oral Expression: The ability to speak English words or sentences so others will understand.

- Speed of Limb Movement: The speed with which movements of the arms or legs can be made; the speed with which the movement can be carried out after it has been initiated.

- Finger Dexterity: The ability to make skillful, coordinated movements of the fingers--may involve equipment, but not equipment controls.

- Color Discrimination: The ability to match or discriminate between colors.

- Written Comprehension: The ability to understand written

sentences and paragraphs.

- Control Precision: The ability to make fine adjustments to a knob or dial

- Math Reasoning: The ability to understand and organize a problem and then to select a mathematical method or formula to solve the problem.

- Written Expression: The ability to write English words or sentences so others will understand.

SEAL Missions and Physical Tasks

The research study produced a long list of missions, mission segments and physical tasks associated with SEAL operations. I selected a number of them for inclusion in this chapter as a means of introducing you to the physical demands placed on SEAL operators. Reviewing this material will also better enable you to contemplate the mindset and attitude necessary for nearly continuous participation in high-risk, dangerous and physically demanding operations.

As you review these missions and physical tasks, you'll note that many are associated with walking long distances in extreme weather conditions while bearing heavy loads of equipment, ammunition, explosives, etc. Some require surface swimming for many miles in frigid waters in both daylight and darkness; and others entail several hours of sub-surface, clandestine infiltration of an enemy controlled area to emplace mines, conduct direct action missions or to perform various reconnaissance-related activities.

I've only listed about 50% of the missions and physical tasks that were included in the study. I contemplated limiting what I showed here even more, for brevity's sake, but decided that the more readers could learn about SEAL operations, the better they could understand the mindset that is associated with these warriors. I doubt that anyone can read what follows and not be impressed by the magnitude of what America demands of its naval commandos. Likewise, learning more about what SEALs do on a frequent basis allows one to fully understand why the physical and mental standards associated with joining the SEAL community are so high. I don't think anyone could argue, after reading this material, that it takes a special breed of man to be able to endure such extreme environments, withstand such punishing conditions, bear such strenuous loads while at the same time executing difficult tasks; oh, and let's not forget, possibly fighting off an enemy and trying to stay alive – they do this day after day, constantly and continuously.

I do want to make one thing perfectly clear; the material that you are about to read has been cleared by appropriate authorities for public dissemination. Nothing you are about to read is classified or otherwise sensitive information from a military intelligence or operational security perspective. That said, an astute reader will note the absence of specific missions and physical tasks more closely aligned with recent SEAL operations in Iraq and Afghanistan. Suffice it to say that the entire special operations community has learned much over the past decade regarding what it takes to operate successfully in both of these very challenging environments and that training programs have been appropriately modified and enhanced.

Navy SEAL Missions and Physical Tasks

- Walk 9 miles over uneven terrain at night, carrying a 125lb. pack (including radios and other gear), in 70°F temperature, to objective; then, retrace steps to extraction point.

- Serve as point man (trail breaker) for an element walking a distance of 26 miles through dense jungle (up and down), in tropical heat and humidity, during a 3 day period, carrying a 60 lbs. pack and weapons.

- Perform a "duck drop," followed by a 21 mile transit (3 hours) in 48°F air temperature, then swim a distance of 2,000 meters in 56°F water carrying a limpet mine and using a Drager underwater breathing apparatus (UBA); return to Zodiac without limpet, then travel 4 miles to extraction point (10 hours total).

- Walk a distance of 26 miles through dense jungle terrain (up and down), in tropical heat and humidity, during a 3 day period, carrying a 40lb. pack, an M-60 (17 lbs.), and 400 rounds of ammunition (40 lbs.).

- Perform a "duck drop," followed by a 14 mile transit in

moderate seas and 65°F air temperature; beach and cache boat, and proceed on foot over 200 meters of strand; enter water and swim 3 miles in current to objective; then, retrace steps to insertion point, during an 8-hour period.

- Travel for 5 hours in an open rubber boat in 40°F air temperature and 30-foot swells; beach the boat, cache/stage the equipment, and change from dry suit into dry clothes; then walk 16 miles during the next 2 nights over uneven terrain carrying an 80lb. pack, sleeping in 2-hour increments, when possible, during a continuous rain.

- Walk a distance of 35 miles from sea level to 4,000 feet, traversing marshy and rocky terrain (frequently on incline below the ridge line), walking at night and laying up during the day, for 3 days, carrying an 80lb. pack, in 30°F to 70°F air temperature.

- Perform a "duck drop" into 39°F water, then conduct a 57 mile over-the-horizon boat transit, then a 2 hour ship attack wearing wet suit and Drager UBA; then, reboard Zodiac for 50 miles, ride to the extraction point.

- Lock out of a submerged submarine, then conduct a 70 mile over-the-horizon transit in a Zodiac in 65°F air temperature (5 hours); enter 58°F water wearing wet suit and Drager UBA, then swim a multi-ship limpet attack that requires 3 1/2 hours under water, re-board Zodiac for 70 mile ride to the extraction point.

- Walk a distance of 12 miles over uneven, snow-covered terrain in 30°F air temperature (crossing two 20-foot streams) during a 2-day period, wearing snowshoes and winter gear, and carrying an 80lb. pack.

- Launch and operate a SEAL delivery vehicle (SDV) for a period of 2 hours, then bottom-out the craft, swim 200 meters to shore carrying 90lbs. of equipment and weights and wearing a dry suit, then proceed overland 1.86 miles to objective; retrace steps to extraction point.

- Walk 37 miles through the desert during a 5-day period, carrying a 100lb rucksack, laying up during the day in 112°F temperature and walking over uneven terrain during nighttime hours (95°F).

- Perform a "duck drop" into 30°F waters then transit 76 miles in a rigid inflatable boat while wearing a dry suit; enter water and swim 600 meters through surf zone to beach while carrying a 50lb pack and weapons; cache boats and change from dry suit to winter gear on beach; hike 2 miles up steep incline with packs; then hike all night for the next 5 nights, laying up during daylight; then, periodically help other platoon members carry downed pilot on stretcher over uneven terrain to extraction point.

- Travel for 6 hours in a Zodiac in 0°F air temperature, then swim 600 meters in 36°F water, crossing the surf zone to the beach; change from wetsuit into winter gear and snow shoes, then walk 1.2 miles over uneven terrain and snow to objective; retrace steps to extraction point (24 hours total).

- Walk a distance of 8 miles through dense jungle (up and down), in tropical heat and humidity, carrying a 40lb pack, an M-60 (17 lbs.), and 400 rounds of ammunition (40 lbs.).

- Perform a rescue drag of a wounded comrade weighing 170 lbs., dragging him by the web gear a distance of 75 meters, with the assistance of 1 other SEAL.

- Climb a 3-tier caving ladder (90 feet) wearing full close quarter battle (CQB) gear and carrying 25 lbs. of weapons and ammunition, pulling self and equipment onto deck of a steel structure.

- Carry a disabled comrade (weighing 170 lbs.) a distance of 200 meters, with the assistance of 2 other SEALs.

- Carry an unconscious SEAL 100 meters through jungle, across 50 feet of sandy beach to water, inflate his flotation device, then tow him seaward for the next 2 hours until rescued.

- Carry a disabled comrade (weighing 170 lbs.) a distance of 500 meters, using a makeshift stretcher, with the assistance of 3 other SEALs.

- Carry a downed and disabled pilot (weighing 170 lbs.) a distance of 100 feet across a beach and through the surf zone.

- Fast rope from an altitude of 50 feet to the heaving deck of a ship while wearing close quarter battle (CQB) gear and carrying 50 lbs. of equipment and weapons.

- Ride in a CRRC for 1 hour to reach a sandy beach; cache the boat and proceed through thick jungle for 500 yards until coming under fire from a numerically superior enemy force; return fire and call in naval gunfire support; return to CRRC to prevent encirclement; then, quickly return to the engagement area through heavy fire to retrieve a critically injured comrade; carry the unconscious SEAL back to the beach, inflate his lifejacket, then tow him seaward for the next 2 hours until picked up by support craft.

- Conduct R&S for 5 days in a jungle environment (95°F temperature and high humidity), while carrying 60 lbs. of equipment and a sniper rifle (movement restricted by thick vegetation to 50 meters per hour.)

- Ride for 3 hours in a riverine patrol boat, then for 1 hour in a CRRC on a jungle river (85°F air temperature and high humidity); climb a 350 foot cliff carrying a rifle and 20 lbs. of ammunition; descend 200 feet through dense vegetation; avoid, return, and eventually suppress intense enemy fire; then, carry wounded comrade 200 yards to extraction site with the assistance of 2 other SEALs.

- Operate a sampan on a jungle river for 4 hours at night; hike through uneven jungle terrain for 1 hour carrying light weapons; locate downed pilot and carry him back to the river with the assistance of 1 other person; return down river for 3 hours then evade intense machine gun fire, direct an air strike to suppress the fire, and successfully reach a forward operating base with the rescued pilot

- Swim on surface a distance of 3.5 miles wearing full close quarter battle (CQB) gear and flotation device and carrying 25 lbs. of weapons/ammunition, in 60°F water; cling to the barnacle-covered leg of an oil platform for 45 minutes (while lead climber scales the structure); then climb a 3 tier caving ladder (90 feet), quietly pulling self and equipment onto deck of platform.

- Crawl for 3 days through a rat and mosquito infested jungle in 90°F temperature and 100% humidity, while carrying a 50lb pack and 25 lbs. of weapons and ammunition; lay up for 2 days, conduct sniper attack, then run .62 miles to extraction point.

- Fast rope to the deck of a salvage ship with 60 lbs. of equipment, then load 6 personnel and their equipment into 2 Zodiacs and launch the boats into 4-foot seas (30°F and 20 kt winds--all personnel wearing dry suits); proceed for 60 miles (10 hours) then take the boats through the surf, caching 1 on the beach (while the other craft and 2 personnel depart); then hump 6.2 miles over uneven terrain with 3 other SEALs (carrying 60 lbs. of equipment each); lay-up for 6 hours, then retrace steps (i.e., 6.2 mile hump, boat through surf zone, and 10 hour ride to extraction point).

- Conduct a 12 day final training exercise in -15°F temperature, covering 37 miles on skis while carrying a 100lb pack.

- Serve as mission specialist riding in an SDV for a period of 3 hours in 68°F water, while wearing a wet suit and MK 15/16 UBA (from an offshore location to within an enemy harbor that is filled with jelly fish); open canopy then swim 50 meters to target to deploy limpets (while jelly fish repeatedly sting exposed lip area); return to SDV and sit among jelly fish in storage compartment as the SDV is operated out of the harbor to the rendezvous location (a total of 8 hours in 68°F water--2 hours of which is in jellyfish infested waters).

- Parachute (static line) into the desert with 150lb packs (day temp 110°F), then walk 47 miles during the next 7 nights.

- Serve as mission specialist riding in an SDV for a period of 3 hours in 65°F water, while wearing a light wet suit; exit SDV then swim 100 meters to shore; change into dry clothes then hump 1.2 miles with 50lb packs in 75°F air temperature; lay up overnight, then hump back to the beach for a 5-hour Zodiac extraction (a total of 2 days with only 3 quarts of water for each person).

- Hike 68 miles in winter gear, carrying a 60lb pack and weapons and completing 5 mini FTXs during a 6 day period (in 25°F temperature with continuous rain and snow). (19%)

- Ride in a Zodiac 6 miles to a rocky beach in 0°F air temperature while wearing winter gear; then, during the next 9 days traverse 50 miles of countryside (uneven terrain, briar patches) by humping (80% of the distance) and cross-country skiing (20%), while carrying a 100lb pack and weapons.

- Parachute into 42°F water wearing wet suits and Drager UBA; tread water for 4 hours waiting for small diesel submarine; enter submerged submarine; travel for 3 days in submarine, then lock out and swim 2 miles on the surface followed by 4 miles underwater (4 hour dive); crawl across 100 meters of rock quay, then swim 3 miles on surface to extraction point.

- Walk 72 miles in 2 1/2 days carrying an M-60, 600 rounds of ammunition, and a rucksack (90 lbs. total), laying up during the day (35°F temp at night and 80°F during the day).

- Perform a "duck drop" from an altitude of 65 feet; repair deflated section of Zodiac, then proceed 40 miles to shore; change into dry clothing and cache boats; swim 1.25 miles (in patrol clothes) towing 30 lbs. of equipment; then climb a 250 foot cliff; remain on top for 2 days, then retrace steps to extraction point (50°F air temperature).

- Perform a "soft-duck drop" then transit 35 miles to surf zone; guide boat through 5 foot surf to shore, then push the boat along the shore line for 8 miles with 3 other SEALs; lay up for 4 days in the jungle, then drive the boat 16 miles to pick up 4 personnel and 800 lbs. of gear; return at slow speed (requiring 8 hours to go the 16 miles), then recon the target for 4 more days before extraction.

- Parachute onto a rocky island then walk 1.2 miles over uneven terrain to shore; retrieve cached kayak, then travel 20 miles in rough seas to objective; travel 6 more miles in kayak, then climb a 2,500-foot mountain (mud and rocks) to the extraction point.

- Navigate a rigid inflatable boat for 10 hours through heavy seas (30°F) with no moon while wearing a dry suit; retrieve personnel who were washed out of boat; fall out of boat and cling to outboard motor (which is operating); climb back into boat and continue operating it; crash boat on rocks, then swim 200 meters through surf zone to beach carrying a 40lb pack and weapons; change into light Goretex outwear (winter gear was lost on rocks) then hump 7 miles over uneven terrain carrying packs and weapons; spend 2 days ashore hiking during the night and laying up during the day, with little sleep, in 35°F air temperature, wind and rain; finally, extraction by vehicle.

It would be safe to say that it takes an immeasurable amount of determination, perseverance, discipline and mental toughness to make it through even the shortest of these missions. All of these men feel the extreme heat or cold, exhaustion, fear and pain that any human would feel under those conditions; the difference is that through the incredibly rigorous training that they put their bodies *and minds* through; they have reached that "next level" of fortitude. You can also elevate your mental toughness and level of resolve to such high-levels. I won't tell you it's easy, I won't tell you it won't take long; but what I can tell you is that IT CAN BE DONE!

What's Your Battlefield?

Assuming that you are not serving in the military or law enforcement, chances are that your battlefield is a bit more sedate and safe than the environments SEALs operate in – and that's a good thing! For many reading this book, the battlefield is the business world, while for others it may be associated with academia or athletics. For many, the battle is happening in their minds as they try to cope with the challenges of health issues or personal relationships. Whatever your particular battle is – your goal – no matter where it will be fought, the main concept that is woven throughout this book is that you should approach it as a SEAL would – to utterly dominate the battle through hard work, intelligent and consistent preparation, confidence and focused actions.

"Fire is the test of gold; adversity, of strong men."

~ Lucius Seneca

Extraordinary Valor

Every Navy SEAL willingly accepts the risks and dangers associated with his chosen profession. Typically operating under a blanket of secrecy, it is a fact of life in the SEAL community that many individual acts of heroism often go unrecognized or are only able to be recognized many years, sometimes decades, later. SEALs have performed heroically in every conflict that the United States has been involved in since the creation of the SEAL teams in 1963. As a result, many SEALs have been awarded various medals for acts of valor. Among this group of heroes are five men whose courage under fire was judged to be so extraordinary that America's highest medal for valor, the **Medal of Honor**, was awarded to them by an act of Congress.

The Medal of Honor is awarded for personal acts of valor above and beyond the call of duty to members of the United States' military. There is a different version of the medal for each official branch of the

U.S. Military; one for the Army, one for the Navy, and one for the Air Force – Marine Corps and Coast Guard personnel receive the Navy version of the medal. The Medal of Honor is usually presented by the President at the White House in a formal ceremony intended to represent the gratitude of the American people, with posthumous presentations made to the primary next of kin. Approximately sixty-percent of the medals awarded during and since World War II have been awarded posthumously.

As previously stated, to date, five Navy SEALs have been awarded America's highest decoration for military valor in combat – three for action in the Vietnam War and one each for actions in Iraq and Afghanistan.

In chronological order these men are Lieutenant Joseph Robert "Bob" Kerrey, Lieutenant Thomas R. Norris, Petty Officer Michael E. Thornton, Lieutenant Michael P. Murphy, and Petty Officer Michael A. Monsoor. They came from different backgrounds and different parts of the country, but they were all united in their desire to serve their country; doing so as part of a close-knit fraternity considered the best of the best. Their actions "above and beyond the call of duty" included ignoring severe wounds in order to save comrades (Kerrey), daring rescues of downed pilots on two separate occasions (Norris), the sacrificing of his life in order to save his comrades (Monsoor and Murphy), and, uniquely, saving the life of a future Medal of Honor recipient (Thornton). In the following chapters, you will find accounts of the acts of valor that resulted in these incredibly brave warriors being awarded the Medal of Honor, as well as the actual citations they received.

Each of these men voluntarily made the decision to serve as Navy SEALs. That decision carries with it a weight like very few others; it means that they accepted the possibility that they may die doing their job. Oh, but it isn't as simple as that! It isn't just about knowing that there is a possibility of death. It means that they are willing to subject themselves to unbelievable levels of training in order to always be able to perform at optimum levels. It means constantly practicing their skills in order to improve upon them. It means learning all that they can about their field of work. It means NEVER GIVING UP. It means choosing to excel. It means going all-in. It means that they are willing to do EVERYTHING in their power to give meaning to their death - should it come to that - and in doing so, also giving meaning to their life.

In the following chapters, you will read more about each of the five Navy SEAL Medal of Honor recipients and their courage while engaged in combat. Their decisions and actions during the specific events for which they were awarded America's highest honor for courage in battle provide superb examples of the tenacity and resolve associated with the mindset that is common amongst all SEAL operators.

"The Spartans do not ask how many are the enemy, but where they are."

~ Plutarch

Lieutenant Joseph R. "Bob" Kerrey

In early March 1969, Lieutenant Kerrey received intelligence about a Viet Cong sapper and political cadre unit located on Hòn Tre Island, located off the coast of the popular South Vietnamese resort of Nha Trang. The communists had been a chronic threat in the area. Thanks to a Viet Cong member who opted to ally himself with American forces, the Kerrey's SEAL unit now had solid intelligence about the makeup and location of the communists' camp, and a raid was planned. In his autobiography, *When I Was a Young Man*, Kerrey wrote that, after he and his men had been ferried close to the island, his plan was to load his team into two rubber boats, "land, hide our boats, hand climb a cliff to where our targets were sleeping, awaken them with force, bind and gag them with tape, and call for a helicopter to remove them to Nha Trang." As you will learn from reading his Medal of Honor citation, things didn't exactly go as planned during the raid!

The night of March 14 was dark, "one of the darkest nights we had in Vietnam," he recalled, which greatly aided them in landing on the island, climbing a 350-foot cliff, and approaching the enemy camp without detection.

The enemy force had split into two groups. Kerrey's team found the first group asleep and quickly bound and gagged them and prepared them for extraction. Kerrey then divided his command, leaving one element to guard their prisoners while he led the other element on a search for the second enemy force.

But instead of being asleep, the second group was moving, and the two sides spotted each other almost simultaneously.

A firefight erupted, with Kerrey being severely wounded by a grenade that exploded at his feet. He quickly applied a tourniquet to his right leg and, despite this and other wounds, calmly directed his element's fire at the enemy's position. He then got on his radio and coordinated supporting cross fire from the SEAL element guarding the prisoners. After about an hour, the enemy fire was sufficiently suppressed that they could call for an extraction. Helicopters soon arrived and Kerrey and other wounded were promptly removed from the area. The prisoners and other SEALs eventually made it safely back to base.

Ultimately, Kerrey's right foot had to be amputated. Kerrey

recalled in his book that it was during his recuperation from his wounds that he was informed that he would be awarded the Medal of Honor. Shortly after getting that news, he was in San Diego visiting his platoon that had just returned from Vietnam, and told them of his reluctance to accept the medal. SEAL Chief Petty Officer Barry Enoch immediately told him he really had no choice, stating, "You must accept this award for everyone who should have been recognized but was not. You must wear it for others."

On May 14, 1970, Lt. (j.g.) Joseph Robert "Bob" Kerrey, together with a number of other servicemen, received the Medal of Honor from President Richard M. Nixon in a White House ceremony.

The President of the United States, in the name of The Congress, takes pleasure in presenting the Medal of Honor to

JOSEPH R. KERREY

Lieutenant (Junior Grade)

United States Navy

For service as set forth in the following

CITATION:

For conspicuous gallantry and intrepidity at the risk of his life above and beyond the call of duty while serving as a SEAL team leader during action against enemy aggressor (Viet Cong) forces. Acting in response to reliable intelligence, Lieutenant Kerrey led his SEAL team on a mission to capture important members of the enemy's area political cadre known to be located on an island in the bay of Nha Trang. In order to surprise the enemy, he and his team scaled a 350-foot sheer cliff to place themselves above the ledge on which the enemy was located. Splitting his team in 2 elements and coordinating both, Lieutenant Kerrey led his men in the treacherous downward descent to the enemy's camp. Just as they neared the end of their descent, intense enemy fire was directed at them, and Lieutenant Kerrey received massive injuries from a grenade which exploded at his feet and threw him backward onto the jagged rocks. Although bleeding profusely and suffering great pain, he displayed outstanding courage and presence of mind in immediately directing his element's fire into the heart of the enemy camp. Utilizing his radioman, Lieutenant Kerrey called in the second element's fire support which caught the confused Viet Cong in a devastating crossfire. After successfully suppressing the enemy's fire, and although immobilized by his multiple wounds, he continued to maintain calm, superlative control as he ordered his team to secure and defend an extraction site. Lieutenant Kerrey resolutely directed his men, despite his near unconscious state, until he was eventually evacuated by helicopter. The havoc brought to the enemy by this very successful mission cannot be over-estimated. The enemy soldiers who were captured provided critical intelligence to the allied effort. Lieutenant Kerrey's courageous and inspiring leadership, valiant fighting spirit, and tenacious devotion to duty in the face of almost overwhelming opposition sustain and enhance the finest traditions of the U.S. Naval Service.

Lieutenant Thomas R. Norris

In early April 1972, two American airmen were trapped deep behind enemy lines in Quang Tri province, Vietnam. One of them, Lt. Col. Iceal "Gene" Hambleton – code name Bat-21B – had managed to evade capture for more than a week. Because Hambleton was an intelligence officer with intimate knowledge of aerial and missile operations, it was doubly imperative he be rescued. Numerous aerial attempts had been made; all had failed. One of those attempts had resulted in a second airman, Lt. Mark Clark (contrary to some accounts, no relation to the World War II general), needing rescue as well, and the calling off of further aerial efforts. The two airmen were then told that the next attempt would be a land rescue up the monsoon-swollen Cam Lo River.

On the night of April 10, 1972, SEAL Lt. Thomas R. Norris, leading a handpicked team of five South Vietnamese Lien Doc Nguoi

Nhia (LDNN), or "soldiers who fight under the sea," similar to Navy SEALs, paddled a sampan more than a mile up the Cam Lo River to get Clark. Clark's trip to the pick-up point was a harrowing one. Twice he was almost spotted by North Vietnamese Army (NVA) patrols. But, at around dawn on the morning of April 11, Clark and Norris linked up and the sampan sped back down the Cam Lo River to their Forward Operating Base (FOB) and safety.

Shortly after Norris's sampan returned, the FOB came under attack by a strong NVA unit that was only repulsed after numerous air strikes were called in. The attack caused several casualties, including the killing of two of the South Vietnamese LDNNs.

On the night of April 12, Norris, together with the remaining three LDNNs, attempted to reach Hambleton. They traveled upriver about 4 kilometers but failed to rendezvous with him. Two of the three South Vietnamese LDNNs were so intimidated by the large number of NVA troops they saw along their route that they refused to return.

On the night of April 13, after receiving updated directions from a Forward Air Controller who had identified Hambleton's location, Norris and LDNN Petty Officer Nguyen Van Kiet, dressed as local fishermen, got into a sampan and headed upriver.

After several harrowing close calls with NVA troops, they found Hambleton; weak and delirious but still alive. Quickly they got him into the sampan and hid him under some bamboo. Now it was a race against time to get back before dawn. Twice they were discovered by North Vietnamese troops. The first time they managed to escape downriver before the patrol could fire at them. The second time they found themselves cut off by an enemy unit with a heavy machine gun. Norris radioed for an air strike. Soon seven airplanes from the USS Hancock arrived, and their attacks enabled Norris to resume his downriver journey.

With the sun high overhead and dodging enemy fire from the other side of the river, Norris and Kiet returned Bat-2 to the FOB. Hambleton's ordeal was finally over.

The U.S. Navy awarded Petty Officer Nguyen Van Kiet the Navy Cross, the only South Vietnamese Navy member to be so honored. On March 6, 1976, in a White House ceremony, President Gerald Ford presented Lieutenant Norris with the Medal of Honor. In an interesting twist to this story, if it hadn't been for the actions of a fellow SEAL, Petty Officer Michael Thornton, Norris might not have lived to receive it. You'll learn more about this is in the next chaper!

The President of the United States, in the name of The Congress, takes pleasure in presenting the Medal of Honor to

THOMAS R. NORRIS

Lieutenant

United States Navy

For service as set forth in the following

CITATION:

Lieutenant Norris completed an unprecedented ground rescue of 2 downed pilots deep within heavily controlled enemy territory in Quang Tri Province. Lieutenant Norris, on the night of 10 April, led a 5-man patrol through 2,000 meters of heavily controlled enemy territory, located 1 of the downed pilots at daybreak, and returned to the Forward Operating Base (FOB). On 11 April, after a devastating mortar and rocket attack on the small FOB, Lieutenant Norris led a 3-man team on 2 unsuccessful rescue attempts for the second pilot. On the afternoon of the 12th, a forward air controller located the pilot and notified Lieutenant Norris. Dressed in fishermen disguises and using a sampan, Lieutenant Norris and 1 Vietnamese traveled throughout that night and found the injured pilot at dawn. Covering the pilot with bamboo and vegetation, they began the return journey, successfully evading a North Vietnamese patrol. Approaching the FOB, they came under heavy machinegun fire. Lieutenant Norris called in an air strike which provided suppression fire and a smoke screen, allowing the rescue party to reach the FOB. By his outstanding display of decisive leadership, undaunted courage, and selfless dedication in the face of extreme danger, Lieutenant Norris enhanced the finest traditions of the U.S. Naval Service.

Petty Officer Michael E. Thornton

About six months after his rescue of Bat-21, in late October 1972, Lt. Thomas R. Norris was even deeper behind enemy lines. This time he was leading a team that included SEAL Petty Officer Second Class Michael E. Thornton and three South Vietnamese commandos on a high risk/high reward reconnaissance mission of the Cua Viet River military base that had been captured by the NVA.

The team was ferried up the South China Sea the night of Oct. 30, 1972, and landed on a beach believed close to the base. The team stealthily entered the enemy base – and quickly discovered that instead of being in the Cua Viet River base, they were dropped north of the Demilitarized Zone border separating South and North Vietnam, and that they were reconnoitering a large NVA base!

The team continued its mission and returned to the beach early on the morning of Oct. 31 to await exfiltration. As they waited, an NVA patrol wandered close. Before Norris or Thornton could stop him, the South Vietnamese commander ordered two of his commandos to capture the patrol. Instead, a firefight broke out, attracting more NVA troops. The next thing Norris and Thornton knew, they were in a fight for their lives in a tactical situation that could only be described as a disaster about to get worse.

Norris was hit in the face and part of his forehead was shot off, exposing his brain. Ignoring the hail of enemy fire, Thornton dashed up and grabbed his lieutenant, who he thought was dead. Amazingly, Norris was still alive.

The team retreated to the sea, where Thornton, wounded across his back and legs by a grenade, inflated Norris's life vest and the vest of one of the commandos, who also had been wounded. After inflating his own vest, Thornton began swimming the two wounded men out to sea for rendezvous with their support craft.

The trio's ordeal lasted hours. Thornton saw one support craft leave the area after having picked up the South Vietnamese commander, who had swum ahead and informed the crew that he was the only survivor. But a second support craft manned by fellow SEAL Woody Woodruff remained in the area, spotted the trio, and rescued them.

Though it would take numerous operations and years to

recuperate, miraculously Norris survived. On Oct. 15, 1973, Petty Officer Second Class Michael Thornton received his Medal of Honor from President Richard Nixon. Norris was there to witness it. And, when Norris received his Medal of Honor in 1976, Thornton had the distinction of becoming the only Medal of Honor recipient to save the life of a fellow recipient.

The President of the United States, in the name of The Congress, takes pleasure in presenting the Medal of Honor to

MICHAEL E. THORNTON

Petty Officer

United States Navy

For service as set forth in the following

CITATION:

For conspicuous gallantry and intrepidity at the risk of his life above and beyond the call of duty while participating in a daring operation against enemy forces. Petty Officer Thornton, as Assistant U.S. Navy Advisor, along with a U.S. Navy lieutenant serving as Senior Advisor, accompanied a 3-man Vietnamese Navy SEAL patrol on an intelligence gathering and prisoner capture operation against an enemy-occupied naval river base. Launched from a Vietnamese Navy junk in a rubber boat, the patrol reached land and was continuing on foot toward its objective when it suddenly came under heavy fire from a numerically superior force. The patrol called in naval gunfire support and then engaged the enemy in a fierce firefight, accounting for many enemy casualties before moving back to the waterline to prevent encirclement. Upon learning that the Senior Advisor had been hit by enemy fire and was believed to be dead, Petty Officer Thornton returned through a hail of fire to the lieutenant's last position; quickly disposed of 2 enemy soldiers about to overrun the position, and succeeded in removing the seriously wounded and unconscious Senior Naval Advisor to the water's edge. He then inflated the lieutenant's lifejacket and towed him seaward for approximately 2 hours until picked up by support craft. By his extraordinary courage and perseverance, Petty Officer Thornton was directly responsible for saving the life of his superior officer and enabling the safe extraction of all patrol members, thereby upholding the highest traditions of the U.S. Naval Service.

Lieutenant Michael P. Murphy

On the night of June 27, 2005, Lt. Michael P. Murphy, a Long Island native who had turned his back on a promising law career to become a SEAL, and his team, including Petty Officers Second Class Marcus Luttrell, Matthew G. Axelson, and Danny P. Dietz, boarded the MH-47 Chinook from the Army's 160th Special Operations Aviation Regiment – the Night Stalkers – to conduct their part in Operation Red Wings, an operation designed to stop insurgents from disrupting the upcoming national elections in Afghanistan. Theirs was a special reconnaissance mission aimed at locating Ahmad Shah, who led a guerrilla group called the Mountain Tigers and was aligned with the Taliban and other militant groups operating close to the Pakistani border.

Discovering their initial observation site to be unsuitable due to fog, they moved to a second location where, at about noon, their mission was compromised when they were discovered by three goatherds leading their goats. As there was no evidence they were insurgents, they were allowed to go.

The SEALs moved to a third location, but about two hours after being discovered, they were attacked from the high ground behind them by Ahmad Shah and his men.

A running firefight down the mountain slope ensued. The SEALs' goal was to reach the village in the valley far below and turn a hut into a fortress where they would fight off Shah and his men until reinforcements arrived.

The SEALs stopped their descent only long enough to return fire and try to communicate with Bagram [a U.S. base and airfield in Afghanistan]. But they were in a communications "dead zone," unable to establish two-way contact.

Meanwhile, Shah used his advantage in superior numbers and high ground to keep up constant pressure. Dietz was killed, and the others all wounded.

When Murphy, Luttrell, and Axelson reached their latest defensive position, Murphy took out his Iridium satellite phone. The only way Murphy could connect with the communication satellites above, however, was to expose himself to enemy fire. He moved out from protective cover and in plain sight of the enemy hit the speed-dial button on the phone.

With AK-47 bullets ricocheting around him, Murphy said, "My men are taking heavy fire ... we're getting picked apart. My guys are dying out here ... we need help."

An AK-47 round struck him in the back and burst through his chest; the impact knocked Murphy forward and caused him to drop his rifle and phone. Somehow, he managed to reach down and pick both up. After listening on the phone for another moment, he replied, "Roger that, sir. Thank you." Then he hung up and staggered back to his fellow SEALs.

Rescue was on the way.

They were SEALs, but they were not supermen. Murphy was soon hit again. The concussion from an RPG explosion knocked Luttrell down the slope, an event that ultimately helped save his life, making him the only survivor of the ordeal. Luttrell's last sight of Axelson was of him using his sidearm; Axelson had three magazines left for his pistol. When a search party found his body days later, only one magazine remained unused.

The initial rescue attempt itself ended in disaster. A Chinook helicopter carrying 8 SEALs and 8 Army Night Stalkers was hit by an RPG. All personnel aboard were killed.

Axelson, Dietz, and Luttrell were awarded the Navy Cross. On Oct. 22, 2007, in a ceremony in front of his parents, President George W. Bush posthumously awarded the Medal of Honor to Lt. Michael

P. Murphy.

The President of the United States, in the name of The Congress, takes pride in presenting the Medal of Honor to

MICHAEL P. MURPHY

Lieutenant

United States Navy

For service as set forth in the following

CITATION:

For conspicuous gallantry and intrepidity at the risk of his life above and beyond the call of duty as the leader of a special reconnaissance element with Naval Special Warfare Task Unit Afghanistan on 27 and 28 June 2005. While leading a mission to locate a high-level anti-coalition militia leader, Lieutenant Murphy demonstrated extraordinary heroism in the face of grave danger in the vicinity of Asadabad, Konar Province, Afghanistan. On 28 June 2005, operating in an extremely rugged enemy-controlled area, Lieutenant Murphy's team was discovered by anti-coalition militia sympathizers, who revealed their position to Taliban fighters. As a result, between 30 and 40 enemy fighters besieged his four-member team. Demonstrating exceptional resolve, Lieutenant Murphy valiantly led his men in engaging the large enemy force. The ensuing fierce firefight resulted in numerous enemy casualties, as well as the wounding of all four members of the team. Ignoring his own wounds and demonstrating exceptional composure, Lieutenant Murphy continued to lead and encourage his men. When the primary communicator fell mortally wounded, Lieutenant Murphy repeatedly attempted to call for assistance for his beleaguered teammates. Realizing the impossibility of communicating in the extreme terrain, and in the face of almost certain death, he fought his way into open terrain to gain a better position to transmit a call. This deliberate, heroic act deprived him of cover, exposing him to direct enemy fire. Finally achieving contact with his Headquarters, Lieutenant Murphy maintained his exposed position while he provided his location and requested immediate support for his team. In his final act of bravery, he continued to engage the enemy until he was mortally wounded, gallantly giving his life for his country and for the cause of freedom. By his selfless leadership, courageous actions, and extraordinary devotion to duty, Lieutenant Murphy reflected great credit upon himself and upheld the highest traditions of the United States Naval Service.

Petty Officer Michael A. Monsoor

In April 2006, Mike Monsoor's 19-man SEAL platoon was deployed to Ramadi, Iraq, and assigned to the Mulaab area, one of the most dangerous neighborhoods in Ramadi. Grafitti on building walls boasted that it was "the graveyard of the Americans."

When he wasn't patrolling on the mean streets of Ramadi, Monsoor, who was the team's heavy weapons machine gunner and communicator, was above them – stationed in rooftop sniper posts. There, acting in his role as a communications specialist, he spotted enemy positions and called in supporting fire.

On Sept. 29, 2006, U.S. Army Colonel Sean MacFarland, the commander of troops in Ramadi, launched Operation Kentucky Jumper, a combined coalition battalion clearance and isolation operation in southern Ramadi using integrated American and Iraqi forces.

Monsoor's assignment was to serve as the machine gunner for a combined-force team of four SEALs and eight Iraqi army soldiers tasked to serve as a sniper overwatch element guarding the western flank of a unit sweeping the area. The SEAL/Iraqi team quickly found a rooftop location that gave them a good field of view and as much defensive security as possible.

Using tactical periscopes to scan over the walls for enemy activity, they soon spotted a group of four armed insurgents conducting reconnaissance for follow-on attacks of the U.S./Iraqi ground force moving through the area. The snipers promptly engaged them, killing one and wounding another. Not long after, another mutually supporting SEAL/Iraqi army team killed another enemy fighter. After these two actions, area residents who supported the insurgents began blocking off the streets around the teams with rocks. The purpose was twofold: to warn away civilians and to identify the location of the sniper teams for the insurgents.

The first attack occurred in the early afternoon, when a vehicle loaded with armed insurgents charged their position. Though the SEALs and Iraqis successfully repulsed the assault, they knew the insurgents would follow up with additional attacks. Despite this risk, the men stayed with the mission and refused to evacuate.

The SEAL lieutenant in charge repositioned his men, placing

Monsoor with his heavy machine gun on the roof outcrop that overlooked the most likely avenue of attack.

Monsoor was using a tactical periscope when an insurgent on the street managed to get close enough to hurl a hand grenade up onto the roof. The grenade hit Monsoor in the chest and bounced onto the rooftop. Monsoor was just a couple of steps away from the exit door. He could have leaped through it to safety. But there were three other SEALs and eight Iraqi soldiers nearby, and no time to throw the grenade over the side of the building.

Monsoor shouted "Grenade!" and as he threw himself onto the grenade, it detonated. Shrapnel from the explosion hit the two SEALs closest to him, wounding them. But Monsoor's body had absorbed most of the blast. Medical evacuation was immediately requested, and within minutes the three wounded were carried away. Monsoor was still alive when he arrived at the field hospital. But his wounds were mortal. Thirty minutes after he had acted to save the lives of those with him, 25-year-old Michael Monsoor died.

On April 8, 2008, at a White House ceremony in front of his parents, President George W. Bush posthumously awarded the Medal of Honor to Petty Officer Monsoor.

The President of the United States, in the name of The Congress, takes pride in presenting the Medal of Honor to

MICHAEL A. MONSOOR

Petty Officer

United States Navy

For service as set forth in the following

CITATION:

For conspicuous gallantry and intrepidity at the risk of his life above and beyond the call of duty as automatic weapons gunner for Naval Special Warfare Task Group Arabian Peninsula, in support of Operation IRAQI FREEDOM on 29 September 2006. As a member of a combined SEAL and Iraqi Army Sniper Overwatch Element, tasked with providing early warning and stand-off protection from a rooftop in an insurgent held sector of Ar Ramadi, Iraq, Petty Officer Monsoor distinguished himself by his exceptional bravery in the face of grave danger. In the early morning, insurgents prepared to execute a coordinated attack by reconnoitering the area around the element's position. Element snipers thwarted the enemy's initial attempt by eliminating two insurgents. The enemy continued to assault the element, engaging them with a rocket-propelled grenade and small arms fire. As enemy activity increased, Petty Officer Monsoor took position with his machine gun between two teammates on an outcropping of the roof. While the SEALs vigilantly watched for enemy activity, an insurgent threw a hand grenade from an unseen location, which bounced off Petty Officer Monsoor's chest and landed in front of him. Although only he could have escaped the blast, Petty Officer Monsoor chose instead to protect his teammates. Instantly and without regard for his own safety, he threw himself onto the grenade to absorb the force of the explosion with his body, saving the lives of his two teammates. By his undaunted courage, fighting spirit, and unwavering devotion to duty in the face of certain death, Petty Officer Monsoor gallantly gave his life for his country, thereby reflecting great credit upon himself and upholding the highest traditions of the United States Naval Service.

Life-Changing Decisions

The fact that you are reading this book probably means that you want to change the current direction of your life in some way. Perhaps you want to achieve a goal that is very challenging. Or, maybe you seek to elevate your level of success in some aspect of your personal or professional life. Whatever it is you are seeking or desiring to accomplish, taking the first step in the journey toward accomplishing it is often the most difficult. Making life-changing decisions is not easy for most people to do, which often leads to procrastination, indecision and, of course, the resulting lack of change, progress or success.

So, if you are ready to change one or more aspects of your life, the first step is to make the decision to change and commit to that decision. The type of commitment I'm talking about here is the unbreakable one that comes from deep in your heart, gut and mind, and is accountable only to yourself.

At some point prior to applying for admission to BUD/S, every man who has ever worn the Trident had to decide if he truly wanted to become a Navy SEAL, and if he was really willing to subject himself to the long and incredibly difficult journey associated with becoming a member of the SEAL brotherhood. More than a few have told me that they thought about this for several years before they finally decided to make the commitment and volunteer to enter the SEAL training pipeline. The lesson here is that even some of the most self-confident and decisive people are often challenged by doubt, fear of failure and other factors that result in procrastination and indecision; but at some point, they realized that the decision to take action had to happen and that only they could make it happen!

Once the decision to take action is made, there is a logical sequence of thought processes and steps to take that can help a person achieve his or her goals. These steps include conducting a personal assessment, finding supportive people who can help you, setting goals or objectives and establishing a plan to achieve them, and of course, taking the actions necessary to follow the plan until success is achieved.

The following chapters will serve as a guide for doing all of the above. You will learn some basic techniques and be exposed to some simple and time-tested concepts related to personal development and the achievement of one's goals. Approach this material with an open mind and evaluate how it can help you accomplish whatever it is that you aspire to.

Assess Yourself

Assuming that there is some aspect of your life that you want to change, it is a given that you will have to change your mindset or attitude to accomplish this. This process should be initiated by conducting an assessment of yourself; your interests, desires, goals, strengths, weaknesses, skills and abilities. The information gained while conducting a personal assessment can be of great help as you establish a plan that will help you achieve or attain whatever it is that you've set as a goal or objective.

Many of us lead very busy lives. It is easy to get swept up in the daily rush, behaviors and actions that, while on the surface seem logical and productive, may actually be preventing you from achieving your goals. You should contemplate the fact that <u>consistent action without reflection enslaves a person to habit</u>, and this is what has led many people to get stuck on what I refer to as the "wheel of mediocrity."

This *wheel* I am alluding to is similar to something we've all seen in the past; the circular-shaped ladders that are placed in squirrel and hamster cages so these creatures can exercise. I am sure you are grasping the point I am trying to convey. The only way to get off the wheel of mediocrity and actually move forward is to conduct an honest assessment of what got you on it in the first place.

Why Should I Assess Myself?

After reading the previous paragraph, I doubt that anyone will resist or doubt the value of conducting a personal assessment. I also think that perhaps some additional perspective on the purpose and value of this exercise would be beneficial. Below you will find some added insights into the question: "Why should I assess myself?"

A personal assessment will help you to:

- Evaluate where you are in relation to where you want to be.

- Identify where your time and effort is being allocated.

- Determine productive and unproductive periods of time and effort.

- Identify aspects of your life which have progressed or regressed.

- Identify habits, actions and inaction relative to various aspects of your life.

- Identify the aspects of your life you are most passionate about.

- Identify the aspects of your life you do not like or enjoy.

- Identify people who add or detract value, stability, peace or harmony to or from your life.

- Identify the changes necessary to enable you to achieve your goals.

Reflecting on the results of such an assessment can provide awareness and insight into your cycle of daily activities, habits, actions and inactions (in some instances, <u>what you aren't doing</u> can be more harmful to your overall success and happiness). This reflection, if conducted in an honest manner, can help you focus in on what is helping you achieve your goals and what is not.

The concept of continuous assessment and reflection is ubiquitous in the SEAL community. After the conclusion of every major training event or combat operation, the participants engage in various forms of debriefing, which includes honest discussion on what worked well and what did not during the evolution. This is how SEALs continually refine their tactics and operational techniques. This model works as well for the evaluation and refinement of people's personal and professional lives, as it does for special operations units like the SEAL teams. Following are actual steps and general guidelines associated with this technique.

Personal Assessment Steps

1. **Schedule Time.** Conducting an assessment of your personal or

professional life takes time and it is best to schedule a window of time during which you can be 100% focused on this exercise. If you have the luxury of taking a day off and going to some place where you can be alone, do so. Eliminating distractions of any kind can help you remain focused as you isolate the attitudes and activities that are helping or hampering your success or happiness. If you cannot take a day to do this, consider getting up early, before anyone else in your family awakens, so you can assess and reflect in a quiet environment. The environment in which you do this assessment has much to do with the quality of the results it will produce. Set yourself up for success by eliminating distractions and by providing ample time to allow you to focus solely on your personal situation.

2. Take Notes. You will need to reflect on the thoughts and ideas you have during the assessment, and it is almost impossible for most people to do this without writing them down. You don't have to use a standard format or template to do this; the important point is that you collect and preserve your thoughts in an organized, comprehensible manner so they can be accessed for future study and reflection. These notes will also serve as the foundation for goal-setting and behavioral modification plans that you'll be creating, so make sure that you plan to utilize some method of note-taking!

3. Priority of Focus. Only you know which aspect of your life you most want to change. It is best to select an aspect to focus on during an assessment. In cases where you have several aspects of your life that you feel merit scrutiny and reflection, you should list them and prioritize them so you attack them in a logical progression. For example, you may decide that while your career needs to be assessed, doing so without first assessing various elements of your personal life may not be effective. Most people find this prioritization process very helpful in ensuring that their personal assessments are executed in a thorough "whole person" manner. Some of the major aspects of a person's life are listed below;

- Personal

- Family

- Professional/Career

- Financial

- Spiritual

- Friends and other relationships

4. Ask Hard Questions. A personal assessment will produce effective and actionable results *only* if you are willing to ask yourself hard and penetrating questions; and, of course, answer them with complete honesty. It would be impossible to list a standard menu of questions that would apply to everyone who will read this book; so instead, I've listed some that I do think will apply to almost everyone's personal situation.

- If I was asked to describe my life in 10 words or less, what words would I choose?

- What aspects of my life am I happy with?

- What aspects of my life am I unhappy with?

- What obstacles are keeping me from doing what I want to do?

- If money was not a factor, I'd be most happy doing _____.

- If it was possible, I would never do _____ again.

- The most important thing that is missing in my life is _____.

5. Be Honest With Yourself. Conducting a personal assessment can be an intense and highly emotional experience – assuming that it is conducted with complete honesty. It is critical that you be willing to confront reality and tell yourself the truth throughout the assessment, because the first step in changing your life is recognizing what your life consists of. You don't have to share your thoughts with anyone else if you don't want to, but you do have to have an honest conversation with yourself. It may not be an enjoyable experience for you, but ultimately you may deem this the most important conversation you've ever had!

6. Commit to Making a Change. Achieving your goals typically means that you have to change various patterns of ideas, beliefs and behaviors that exist in your daily life. Be realistic, unless you break free from the attitudes and activities that led you to your current state, there's little chance of you achieving your goals. In other words, you have to commit to changing whatever it is that is holding you back or otherwise hindering your progress.

True commitment is hard work and is not to be confused with mere involvement. To ensure that you fully understand what I mean by the word commitment, I'll pass on a great anecdote that I once heard a SEAL Senior Chief Petty Officer tell a young SEAL lieutenant. The officer was about to lead about a dozen of his men on a mission deep into enemy-controlled territory. The Senior Chief was making sure that the officer and his senior enlisted SEAL had made all of the appropriate arrangements for fire support, emergency extraction and escape and evasion plans in case the operation became compromised, etc. Finding some details that were not as thoroughly taken care of as he thought necessary, the Senior Chief took the officer aside and said, "Sir, you must remember that once you and your men fly away in the helicopter, all of us back here in the command post will be involved in this operation. But, the minute that bird lands and your feet touch the ground, you and your men are committed to it. There's a big difference, sir, between being involved in this operation and being committed to it. If you want to do everything possible to ensure that your guys survive this operation, you need to ratchet your level of commitment up a few notches starting now. I suggest that you and your chief take another look at your contingency plans and make sure they are really to the point that you're willing to bet your life and the lives of your men on them, because there's a good chance that you'll have to do just that."

The lesson here is that while others may be involved in helping you achieve your goals, you're not likely to accomplish much unless you are truly committed to making things happen. You'll recall that in a previous chapter, part of the purpose of BUD/S was to instill several core values into each man who would ultimately go on to serve as a Navy SEAL. Three of those core values apply when making the commitment to change, and I list them here so that you can reflect upon them as you contemplate the level of commitment necessary to improve your life or achieve your goals. These core values are:

- Whatever needs to happen, must be *made* to happen.

- Luck is good, but preparation is better.

- Never make excuses.

7. Set Goals. Once you know what you want to achieve, you must establish measurable, prioritized goals. This topic is covered in detail in a subsequent chapter.

8. Take Action. The critical ingredient in changing your life and achieving your goals is taking action and literally making things happen on a daily basis. This topic will also be addressed in a subsequent chapter.

The self-assessment is only the beginning, but once you've done it, you will have taken the first step toward accomplishing your goal.

This self-assessment will ready your mind for the arduous road ahead as you embark on your new mission to accomplish your set goals. It is important to know that, although YOU will have to do the majority of the hard work, make the hard decisions, and ultimately change your mindset, you don't have to do it alone. If you look closely, I'm sure that you will find people around you who, knowingly or unknowingly, can aid you in your endeavor. There are probably people around you who have accomplished what you seek to accomplish; ASK THEM FOR HELP!

The life which is unexamined is not worth living.

~ Plato

Get a Mentor

Just about every SEAL will admit that early in their military careers, they found a role model or mentor (often referred to as a "Sea Daddy") within their unit, a person they looked at and thought to themselves "I want to be like him." Typically, this person is one of the more seasoned operators within the unit, and these experienced SEALs are always very willing to share their experiences and "tricks of the trade" with their younger teammates.

When looking to improve an aspect of your life, finding a mentor, someone you wish to emulate, is the most efficient way to achieve your goal. Find someone who has already achieved what you aspire to. Watch them, observe how they act, what they do. Most importantly, establish a solid relationship with them. Then, when the time is right, pose the questions you would like to have answered. I'm sure they would be more than willing to share their experiences with you. I want to emphasize one major point – Navy SEALs cannot achieve the highest levels of effectiveness as special operators by themselves – they need solid leadership and the counsel and advice of a wise-elder who has 'been-there-done-that' and lived to tell about it. I don't think the concept of having a mentor is new to most readers. I'd bet that most were literally taught as young children that it was important to find a role model and to seek various sources of wisdom and guidance. Most often, this was achieved through our relationships with teachers, athletic coaches, the leaders of youth and religious activities and, of course, our parents. Ideally, we'd leverage their experience and guidance and weave it into various aspects of our lives.

The SEAL community places much value on the mentoring of new frogmen, and it is considered one's duty to serve as a mentor once you've attained a level of experience that warrants it. After my military career was over, I began to study high-achievers in other walks of life and one common denominator always surfaced among highly successful athletes, entrepreneurs and business leaders, lawyers or real estate tycoons – the presence and influence of mentors. In fact, it appeared to me that those who had sought the guidance and assistance of mentors early in their careers usually achieved significant success at an earlier age than those who waited until their 40s, 50s or later to seek mentoring.

Benefits of Having a Mentor

The benefits of having a mentor are numerous and I could easily write several chapters on this topic. Instead, I will simply list what I feel are the major benefits of having a mentor.

Having a mentor will enable you to:

- Learn and develop from their past experiences.

- Be exposed to different concepts, perspectives and experiences.

- Receive honest feedback and advice.

- Seek input on your ideas and plans.

- Gain access to your mentor's network of contacts.

- Learn specific skills and knowledge that are relevant to your goals.

Role Models, Mentors and Coaches

SEALs have a combination of mentors, role models and coaches helping them develop personally and professionally during their formative years. I'm sure that many readers have also had one or more helping them at various points in their lives. I think it is important to discuss the distinct similarities and differences between the three types of people that can have a huge impact on your life and level of achievement.

When comparing the characteristics of role models, mentors and coaches, it is easy to identify some commonalities. Each will be a person that you would like to emulate to some degree. They will all possess knowledge that is valuable and which they can teach you. In most instances, the lessons they can teach you will not be found in a textbook or other method of study. Typically, the wisdom and guidance these people can give you stems from their own life experiences. Most often, they will convey this to you during the frequent conversations you will have with them.

The following question naturally arises...whom should you choose? Making the right choice will determine your interaction with the individual.

Role Model

A role model is usually someone who has achieved things or possesses skills that we admire. Role models are typically observed from a distance, and there's a high probability that you'll never actually meet or interact with your role model. Ask any SEAL who his role model is and he'll likely give you the name of a legendary frogman from a past era of Navy Special Warfare, or a SEAL who has distinguished himself in the more recent conflicts in Iraq and Afghanistan. Young people often see high-achieving athletes, singers and actors as role models. Adults typically have role models for various aspects of their personal and professional lives. Emulating the characteristics and attributes of a role model is positive and can help a person stay motivated during his or her quest for excellence and achievement. The major limitation of a role model is that there's usually no interaction between them and the individual that views them as such. It's typically an "observational" form of relationship.

Mentor

A mentor is usually a person that you'd be able to interact with on a regular basis. Unlike the role model relationship, you will typically have frequent access to your mentor and will receive a good amount of advice and guidance from him or her. Mentors are usually, but not always, working in the same industry or occupation that you are. They are usually on the same path that you are on, but have obviously covered more ground, and, as a result, have learned lessons that can be passed on to you. A lot of value is gained by observing your mentor in action, but the opportunity for frequent discussions in which you can ask the mentor questions and seek advice on specific situations or issues is priceless!

Coach

Most of us have had some type of coach during our life. Whether it was related to athletics, music, dance, martial arts, academics or business; or in a specific trade such as carpentry or welding, the coach was the person that evaluated our ability and skill level and gave us advice on how to become more competent and effective. The concept of having a coach applies to all walks of life and any goal or vision that any reader of this book could possibly have. You will have a close relationship with your coach, and the focus is on specific skills or tasks that can be isolated, refined and practiced to a desired level of proficiency.

Asking for Help

Now that you understand the differences between role models, mentors and coaches, contemplate whether you already have all three of them in your life. If you do, reflect on whether or not they are the right people for that role and if they are having a positive impact on your life and goals. It is perfectly acceptable to decide a change is needed in any or all of these influences. If you do not have these people in your life at this time, consider what your situation is and what your goals are and look for individuals who possess the knowledge and experience that you would benefit from. Once you identify the appropriate individuals, form a plan for how you will tactfully and respectfully approach them and ask for their help. My experience has been that high-achievers and subject matter experts are typically very willing to share their time and knowledge with those who are truly committed to learning.

Asking for the Right Kind of Help

It is important to ask for the appropriate kind of help from the appropriate individual. Mentors are typically most effective when you leverage their experience and knowledge to help shape your attitude, perspective and behavior. Coaches, on the other hand, are often not as experienced as those qualified to serve as mentors, but they are very adept at teaching you a specific skill. For example, a new SEAL may seek mentoring from the Chief Petty Officer that is leading his platoon. Once the relationship and mutual trust develops, the young SEAL may open up and seek the Chief's advice regarding a very private and personal issue such as marital or family problems, or perhaps he's trying to decide whether to reenlist or leave the Navy and go to college, etc. This is an appropriate level of interaction for a mentor/mentee relationship.

On the other hand, if that same SEAL was having some kind of problem or issue during CQB training, he would probably not seek assistance or additional instruction from the Chief. Instead, he'd seek advice and remedial training from the SEALs who are actually serving as CQB instructors. These men may not have the same level of experience and wisdom that enables the Chief to effectively counsel the SEAL on family issues or other personal matters, but they are indeed subject matter experts in the science and art of combat shooting. They will surely have the solutions to any shooting-related problem this SEAL may be having. I think you get the point I am trying to convey; don't ask a mentor for coaching on specific skills and tasks, and don't seek mentoring from those serving in roles more focused on coaching. Some people can provide both forms of assistance but not often in my experience. The key is to seek the right kind of help from the right person!

"Better than a thousand days of diligent study is one day with a great teacher."

~ Japanese proverb

Setting Goals

Countless studies have revealed that the human brain is instinctively a goal-seeking organism. It is beyond debate that establishing goals and embedding them in the subconscious mind results in a more focused, determined and persistent individual. In other words, when you consciously reflect upon goals you want to achieve, write them down and review them on a daily basis, they begin to occupy a prominent position in your subconscious mind. This causes your mind to think of these goals on a continuous basis without the individual even knowing that it is happening. I realize that some may be thinking that what they've just read is hype, but I counter their thoughts with this; think about the most successful person you know, one who has risen to great heights in his or her profession or vocation. I'm willing to bet that the individual each of you is thinking about is driven, exceptionally committed and is the embodiment of the old saying, *"he eats, sleeps and breathes _____!"*

Goal-Setting Systems

There are many proven goal-setting systems, methods and techniques that can be used to help you achieve your goals. Some are very simple and others quite sophisticated. You can find hundreds of books devoted to the topic of goal setting. Don't allow this to confuse you or to cause you anxiety about which system or method you should choose. The most important thing to focus on is that you must choose and utilize a goal-setting method or technique. Without this, your chances of devising, prioritizing, attacking and achieving your goals are greatly diminished.

One goal-setting system that is very popular among members of various special operations units is the SMART Goals System. I believe that it was first used in the business world and subsequently adopted by individuals in the U.S. military. I have seen the SMART Goals technique mentioned in many business and personal development books dating back to the 1930s. Conversely, I have never seen this system mentioned in a military-related book or publication that was published prior to the 1980's. At any rate, it is a proven system and the one that I used throughout my military career; and I know for a fact that it is used by many special operators in their professional and personal lives.

There are too many goal-setting systems and methods to list in this chapter. Like anything else, some people will prefer certain types of goal-setting concepts and practices, while others would choose entirely different ones. For the sake of simplicity and conveying the main lesson of this chapter – that you must use a goal-setting process – I am choosing the SMART Goals System, as it is the one that I have personally used to great effect.

The SMART Goals System

This system involves five key elements: a goal that's specific, measurable, attainable, relevant and time-bound.

Specific Goals: This element stresses the need for specific and very detailed goals instead of more broadly defined, general ones. All goals must be clear and unambiguous, without unnecessary adjectives or vague statements. For goals to be specific, they must illustrate exactly what is expected, why is it important, who's involved, where is it going to happen and which attributes are important.

A specific goal will usually answer these questions:

- What: What is the desired end state?

- Why: Specific benefits of accomplishing the goal.

- Who: A list of people directly or indirectly involved in achieving the goal.

- Where: If appropriate to the situation, the locations associated with the goal.

Measurable Goals: All goals must be able to be clearly defined and measured. Goals that can be measured are more easily monitored for progress, need for modification of plans and timeliness. Experienced planners agree that the majority of people or organizations that fail to reach their goals do so because they did not apply an adequate form of measurement to keep track of their progress.

A measurable goal will usually answer questions such as:

- How much?

- How many?

- How will I know when the goal is achieved?

Attainable Goals: This book emphasizes the need for people to engage in "no-limits thinking" and "stretching" beyond real or perceived limitations to accomplish their goals. Most goals of a significant value are in fact "stretch goals" that require the mental toughness and resolve to push through barriers, but the fact remains that they must be attainable. Some people set goals that are too aggressive or challenging, to the point that they become unrealistic or unattainable. The micro-task concept is a very effective technique when setting attainable goals. For example, instead of a person stating they will lose 30 lbs., they should consider stating that they will lose 2 lbs. per week for 15 weeks.

An attainable goal will usually answer these questions:

- Have others already accomplished it?

- How can the goal be accomplished?

- Do you have access to the knowledge, tools and support required to accomplish it?

Relevant Goals: It is important to select goals that actually help you achieve your desired end state. A college professor's goal of completing a marathon may be relevant to his personal life, but it will likely not have any impact on his professional goal of becoming a tenured faculty member. This is a critical concept that you must understand completely! It is imperative that you write down a list of what you really want to achieve and ensure that all other goals, objectives and efforts are relevant to accomplishing it.

A relevant goal can answer yes to these questions:

- If I accomplish this, will my highest and most important goals be reached?

- Is this the right time to do this?

- Does accomplishing this goal enhance my chances of success toward accomplishing my ultimate end-state?

Time-bound Goals: All goals must be associated with specific dates of completion. Aligning a goal with specific dates and time-related milestones instills a sense of urgency and accountability among the people involved in accomplishing it. It also enables the measurement aspect of the SMART Goals Method, as previously discussed. Last, but not least, setting time parameters and due dates is very helpful in ensuring that the progress toward accomplishing a goal is not overtaken by the inevitable emergencies or issues that occur in everyone's lives. When such things happen, having a set timeline enables you to quickly assess how much your plan has been affected and can help you set a new course to regain momentum and get back on track.

A time-bound goal will usually answer these questions:

- When will the goal be achieved?

- What are the intermediate due dates assigned to micro-tasks or smaller objectives?

- What progress must be achieved by next week, six weeks from now, in 90 days, etc.?

- What specific actions am I taking today, this week, for the next 60 days, etc.?

The SMART Goal System has worked for many people, including SEALs and other special operators, and it can work for you. High-achievers in various professions have a bias for action that is always accompanied by the discipline to conduct proper analysis and planning, which, of course, includes setting goals. I know that you have dreams and objectives that you want to accomplish. Creating well-designed goals is the first step in making them happen!

"Our plans miscarry because they have no aim. When a man does not know what harbor he is making for, no wind is the right wind."

~ Lucius Annaeus Seneca

Take Action

During my many years of working with SEALs and members of other special operations forces, I have found that the one thing that separates the very good, solid operators from those recognized as being truly exceptional is that those in the latter group take action to a far greater degree than those in the former.

Every SEAL in an operational unit is very skilled in CQB and the SEAL standard for speed and accuracy places these men among the very best in the world at this skill. However, even among this group of supremely confident warriors, there is an acknowledgement, often unspoken, that some members of the team are shooting at a superior level, and these men become known as the *go-to-guys* during missions requiring split-second, precision shooting. This also applies to other aspects of being a SEAL such as swimming, underwater navigation, and knowledge and employment of highly sophisticated weapons systems and technology.

How do these operators manage to rise above their peers in various skills? In every instance that I am aware of, they achieved this by devoting time toward additional practice and study, sometimes doing so at their own expense. The lesson here is that even within an elite military unit such as the SEALs, there are individuals who decide that they want to excel and exceed the standard levels of training. So, they take action, and whatever it is that they want to become more adept at, they find ways to make it happen.

The main point I'm trying to convey is that whatever your personal situation is, and no matter what kind of organization or system you are operating in, <u>nothing will change unless you take action!</u> If the SEALs mentioned above were satisfied with the CQB training they received from within the SEAL teams during the early 1980s, they would not have asked for permission to attend some civilian-run shooting schools or courses run by other branches of the U.S. armed forces or foreign special operations units. But, because some SEALs did this during the early stages of the integration of CQB into the SEAL mission profile, they were able to absorb some incredibly effective tactics and techniques that not only elevated their personal skills, but were ultimately included into the CQB curriculum that every SEAL is exposed to.

So, whatever it is that you want to achieve, acquire or become more proficient in; you must assume a <u>bias for action</u>. Even if things appear to be difficult and obstacles surface that might threaten your ability to take action, you must proceed, you must move forward and make things happen. Don't become a slave to planning, goal setting or other conceptual or administrative aspect associated with achieving the things you want to achieve, at some point you simply must get started on the path to success. Remember that it is a fundamental law of warfare that "No battle plan survives the first shot," which means that even the best made plans have to be adjusted and modified once situations change. Assessments, setting goals and planning steps to achieve your goals are certainly important, but they will ultimately be useless unless you take action.

There's never a perfect time to take action. For most people, there's always something going on that could easily be used as an excuse or reason why they can't take action. Don't fall into this trap. Do not join or remain in the legions of people who are unsatisfied with their lives or who aspire to higher levels of achievement and success, only to sit idle because of excuses such as:

- My job takes up all of my time.

- I have to spend time with my spouse, children, etc.

- My children aren't adults yet.

- Nobody in my company, family, etc., has ever done this before.

- I'm not sure how my friends will react if I do this.

- I'm not ready to do this yet, but I will be next year.

An example of someone who simply wouldn't sit idle and make excuses is Carlos Moleda, a former Navy SEAL, who took action even after his life plan was irreversibly altered. He was born in Brazil and moved to the U.S. in 1980 at the age of 18. A few years later he joined the Navy and became a Navy SEAL.

In 1989, the United States executed Operation Just Cause, the invasion of Panama, to protect American interests in that nation. While conducting a covert mission to capture Panamanian dictator Manuel Noriega's airplane (to prevent him from fleeing the country), Moleda and his SEAL team were caught in a horrible firefight. Carlos was shot in the leg and spine, which left him paralyzed at the age of 27.

Knowing little about how spinal cord injuries work, Carlos couldn't accept that he would never walk again. Faced with the reality of what his life would be, he probably would have spiraled downward if not for the words of one of his SEAL teammates, who said: "Dude, you are still the same guy. You are still a Navy SEAL," and placed a Trident in Moleda's hand. Those words were the exact push he needed to bring forth all the training he had learned with the SEALs and take action on a new plan for a new way of life.

While rehabilitating in Seattle, he was introduced to adaptive cycling racing; and from that moment on he set his sights on a new goal. Carlos moved to Virginia Beach and started training and preparing his plan to conquer the racing world. After a short time, he was already racing in marathons. He also attended a community college, where he met Sarah Preston. Within a year he and Sarah married, they moved to Phoenix, and they had a son.

Carlos continued to work hard, earned a degree in graphic design, and continued to race. When he heard about a paralyzed man who would be racing in the Ironman World Championships in Kona, Hawaii — a one-day race consisting of a 2.5-mile swim, a 112-mile bike ride and a marathon – he set a new goal for himself. He decided that he would not only race in the Ironman, but he would win the Ironman within 2 years.

The next four years consisted of a whirlwind of rigorous training, many competitions and starting a successful business. Carlos won the 1999 Midnight Sun, took first in the U.S. Handcycling Championships in 1999 and 2000, and won the Ironman World Championships in 1998-99. His success on this race brought about a surge in interest from people who were looking to buy wheelchair sports equipment. His web-design experience coupled with his passion for racing came together when he started High Performance Mobility, one of the first online wheelchair sports outlets. Through his success in the Ironman, he obtained a contract to fill equipment orders for the Challenged Athletes Foundation (CAF), a non-profit that provides funding for equipment, training, programs and events for athletes with disabilities. Carlos also became a CAF spokesperson.

In 2001, Carlos injured his left hip just 2 days before a race. Feeling pressure to do the race due to a sense of responsibility to his sponsors and all his followers, he raced anyway. The race put so much pressure on his hip that after the race, Carlos had to undergo 3 different surgeries and spent almost 3 years recovering. At one point he developed an infection that required 24hour care. After two long years involving constant medical care from nurses, doctors and his wife, he found a specialist for a third surgery. This time it worked. Carlos said the whole experience made him realize that all the success he had achieved had only been possible because of the support of many people.

Carlos returned to racing with a vengeance. He went back to Hawaii and won the 2004 and 2005 Ironman. In 2009 he was part of the first four-man handcycle team that successfully completed the Race Across America, a 3,000-mile race from Oceanside, CA, to Annapolis, MD, in eight days. He continues to race and now runs a successful business worldwide. He is also very involved in programs helping returning injured veterans. I think it is safe to say that Carlos is a superb example of the iron will and resilience SEALs are known for, and that his actions and approach to life after can serve as examples for anyone desiring to overcome difficult challenges.

Let's face it, successful people, those you admire and want to emulate, are usually very action-oriented; like Carlos Moleda, they have a bias for action and are focused on making progress toward their goals. A bias for action does not mean you should act impulsively, rather, having a bias for action simply means you get things moving. This enables you to spend more time executing your plan and refining it as you move forward. You've already learned how to set goals, break them down into smaller micro-goals and try to anticipate obstacles and unforeseen issues that you must adapt to.

You know what to do; now you just have to do it! It is time for action! Join the health club, enroll in the course, sign up for the training, begin the diet, reach out to the people you want to meet or have a better relationship with, schedule the appointment with your boss to discuss your ambitions, create the outline to the book you want to write, book the trip you've always wanted to take; whatever it is that you desire to achieve – TAKE ACTION NOW!

Action expresses priorities.

~ Mahatma Gandhi

Conclusion

I have done my best to provide you with a solid look into the winning mindset of Navy SEALs; how they think and how they approach various situations and tasks, and the reasons why. You should now realize that while these warriors are truly special men, what makes them special is not their physical strength or specific warrior skills; it is what resides in their minds that truly sets them apart from most people.

I've cited examples in which SEALs have persevered under circumstances that would cause the majority of people to simply quit and surrender to the situation facing them. You should close this book knowing that the traits, attitudes and iron will demonstrated by these exceptional warriors are attainable by anyone who desires to have them and has the initiative to put them into action.

You already possess the talent and aptitude to achieve your goals, and you have access to various individuals and resources that can help you get started on your journey to success. The time for inspirational and motivating Navy SEAL stories and anecdotes is done – <u>It is time for YOU to take action!</u>

You know that you alone are responsible for your success; so get going and…

MAKE IT HAPPEN!

Made in the USA
Lexington, KY
19 December 2013